First World War
and Army of Occupation
War Diary
France, Belgium and Germany

31 DIVISION
Headquarters, Branches and Services
Royal Army Ordnance Corps
Deputy Assistant Director Ordnance Services
6 March 1916 - 31 December 1918

WO95/2348/3

The Naval & Military Press Ltd
www.nmarchive.com
Published in association with The National Archives

Published by

The Naval & Military Press Ltd

Unit 10 Ridgewood Industrial Park,

Uckfield, East Sussex,

TN22 5QE England

Tel: +44 (0) 1825 749494

www.naval-military-press.com

www.nmarchive.com

This diary has been reprinted in facsimile from the original. Any imperfections are inevitably reproduced and the quality may fall short of modern type and cartographic standards.

Contents

Document type	Place/Title	Date From	Date To
Heading	WO95/2348-3		
Heading	31st Division Divl Troops D.A. Dir. Ordnance Services Mar 1916-Dec 1918.		
War Diary	Marseilles.	06/03/1916	06/03/1916
War Diary	Abbeville.	08/03/1916	09/03/1916
War Diary	Hallencourt.	17/03/1916	25/03/1916
War Diary	Bus-Les-Artois.	27/03/1916	31/05/1916
Heading	D.A.G. 3rd Echelon. Herewith War Diary for June please.		
War Diary	Bus Les. Artois.	04/06/1916	30/06/1916
Heading	War Diary of D.A.D.O.S. 31st Divin 1st July to 31st July 1916. Vol 5.		
War Diary	Bus Les Artois.	01/07/1916	05/07/1916
War Diary	Ribeaucourt.	06/07/1916	06/07/1916
War Diary	St. Venant.	09/07/1916	14/07/1916
War Diary	Lestrem.	15/07/1916	31/07/1916
Heading	War Diary of D.A.D.O.S. 31st Divn Aug 1916 Vol 6.		
War Diary	Lestrem.	01/08/1916	31/08/1916
Heading	War Diary D.A.D.O.S. 31st Division September 1916. Volume 7.		
War Diary	Bethune.	26/09/1916	30/09/1916
War Diary	Lestrem.	01/09/1916	16/09/1916
War Diary	Bethune.	17/09/1916	25/09/1916
Heading	War Diary D.A.D.O.S. 31st Division October 1916 Volume 8.		
War Diary	Bethune.	01/10/1916	07/10/1916
War Diary	Marieux.	08/10/1916	15/10/1916
War Diary	Authie.	18/10/1916	31/10/1916
Heading	War Diary D.A.D.O.S. 31st Division November 1916 Volume XI.		
War Diary	Authie.	02/11/1916	30/11/1916
Heading	War Diary D.A.D.O.S. 31st Division December 1916 Volume XII.		
War Diary	Authie.	08/12/1916	30/12/1916
Heading	War Diary D.A.D.O.S. 31st Division January 1917 Volume XIII.		
War Diary	Authie.	01/01/1917	09/01/1917
War Diary	Beauval.	11/01/1917	16/01/1917
War Diary	Bernaville.	22/01/1917	25/01/1917
Heading	War Diary D.A.D.O.S. 31st Division February 1917 Volume XIV.		
War Diary	Bernaville.	01/02/1917	18/02/1917
War Diary	Authie.	21/02/1917	28/02/1917
Heading	War Diary D.A.D.O.S. 31st Division. March 1917 Volume XV.		
War Diary	Authie.	01/03/1917	04/03/1917
War Diary	Couin.	05/03/1917	20/03/1917
War Diary	St Venant.	21/03/1917	30/03/1917
Heading	War Diary D.A.D.O.S. 31st Division April 1917 Volume XVI.		

War Diary	St. Venant.	02/04/1917	07/04/1917
War Diary	Bethune.	09/04/1917	18/04/1917
War Diary	Bruay.	19/04/1917	24/04/1917
War Diary	Heripre.	25/04/1917	30/04/1917
War Diary	Marceuil.	30/04/1917	30/04/1917
Heading	War Diary D.A.D.O.S. 31st Division May 1917 Volume XVII.		
War Diary	Maroeuil.	01/05/1917	30/05/1917
Heading	War Diary D.A.D.O.S. 31st Division June 1917 Volume XVIII.		
War Diary	Maroeuil.	01/06/1917	09/06/1917
War Diary	St. Catherine.	10/06/1917	30/06/1917
Heading	War Diary D.A.D.O.S. 31st Division July 1917 Volume XIX.		
War Diary	St Catherine.	01/07/1917	02/07/1917
War Diary	Maroeuil.	04/07/1917	31/07/1917
Heading	War Diary D.A.D.O.S. 31st Division August 1917 Volume XX.		
War Diary	Maroeuil.	01/08/1917	29/08/1917
Heading	War Diary D.A.D.O.S. 31st Division September 1917 Volume XXI.		
War Diary	Maroeuil.	02/09/1917	30/09/1917
Heading	War Diary D.A.D.O.S. 31st Division October 1917. Volume XXII.		
War Diary		02/10/1917	31/10/1917
Heading	War Diary D.A.D.O.S. 31st Division November 1917 Volume XXIII.		
War Diary	Maroeuil.	02/11/1917	07/11/1917
War Diary	Ecurie.	08/11/1917	30/11/1917
Heading	War Diary D.A.D.O.S. 31st Division December 1917. Volume XXIV.		
Miscellaneous	O i/c Records A.O.C this O i/c Section G.H.Q. 3rd Echelon B.E.F.		
War Diary	Ecurie.	01/12/1917	07/12/1917
War Diary	Maroeuil.	08/12/1917	14/12/1917
War Diary	Ecurie.	15/12/1917	02/03/1918
War Diary	Fineques.	03/03/1918	23/03/1918
War Diary	Douchy Les Ayette.	24/03/1918	24/03/1918
War Diary	Humber Camps.	25/03/1918	01/04/1918
War Diary	Lachemn.	02/04/1918	02/04/1918
War Diary	Iinques.	03/04/1918	07/04/1918
War Diary	On The Rd Near Hazebrouck	08/04/1918	11/04/1918
War Diary	Morbequet.	11/04/1918	11/04/1918
War Diary	Wallon Cappell.	12/04/1918	25/04/1918
War Diary	Handighem.	27/04/1918	30/04/1918
Heading	War Diary D.A.D.O.S. 31st Divn. May 1918 Volume XXIX.		
War Diary	Handighem.	02/05/1918	23/05/1918
War Diary	Blaringhem.	24/05/1918	21/06/1918
War Diary	Wallon Capell.	22/06/1918	22/08/1918
War Diary	Hondeghem.	24/08/1918	01/09/1918
War Diary	Caestre.	02/09/1918	10/10/1918
War Diary	Caestre La Creche.	11/10/1918	16/10/1918
War Diary	La Creche to Semmy.	21/10/1918	21/10/1918
War Diary	Lammoy.	23/10/1918	26/10/1918
War Diary	Near Cuerne.	27/10/1918	31/10/1918

War Diary	Near Coutrai Sheet 29 H.20.a.5.3.	01/11/1918	02/11/1918
War Diary	Roncq.	03/11/1918	07/11/1918
War Diary	Coutrai	08/11/1918	08/11/1918
War Diary	Sweveghem.	10/11/1918	12/11/1918
War Diary	Pottelberg.	15/11/1918	21/11/1918
War Diary	St Omer.	25/11/1918	31/12/1918

31ST DIVISION
DIVL TROOPS

D.A.DIR.ORDNANCE SERVICES
MAR 1916-DEC 1918

Instructions regarding War Diaries and Intelligence Summaries are contained in F. S. Regs., Part II. and the Staff Manual respectively. Title pages will be prepared in manuscript.

WAR DIARY

or

~~INTELLIGENCE SUMMARY.~~

(Erase heading not required.)

Army Form C. 2118.

D.A.D.O.S. 31st Div. MARCH. 1916.

Vols 1.2.3

Place	Date	Hour	Summary of Events and Information	Remarks and references to Appendices
			D.A.D.O.S. left PORT SAID 28th on H.M.T. Northland arrived at MARSEILLES Mch 6th 1916.	
MARSEILLES	6th	5 pm	Entrained for ABBEVILLE with Transport Sections of Units to be refitted with Vehicles, horses etc to replace transport left at KANTARA. EGYPT.	
ABBEVILLE	8th	4.30	Arrived. Reported to Ord. HAVRE list of Units comprising Divn	
"	9th		Wire to Base for Warm Clothing, 2nd Blanket also 1st Supplies of Anti Gas Satchels & P.H.G. Helmets.	
HALLENCOURT	11th	5 pm	Good Office & Dump.	
"	12th		Wire to Base for 5050 Caps SD to replace Helmets 28	
"	13		" " " " 18500 P.H. Anti Gas Helmets. Authority 4th Army	
"	13		" " " " 3rd Blanket (30000) Authority Q.O.S. 498a 4-13th Q.	
"	13		Our 1st "Bulk" wire to Base, this being for Service Dress	
"	14		Arrival of 7070 Blankets from Base. – Demanded on 9th	
"	14		Medical Officer of 11th East Lancs. condemns 2 Water Tank Carts in possession of his Regt.	

2353 Wt. W2544/1454 700,000 5/15 D. D. & L. A.D.S.S./Forms/C. 2118.

Instructions regarding War Diaries and Intelligence Summaries are contained in F. S. Regs., Part II. and the Staff Manual respectively. Title pages will be prepared in manuscript.

WAR DIARY
or
INTELLIGENCE SUMMARY.
(Erase heading not required.)

Army Form C. 2118.

Place	Date	Hour	Summary of Events and Information	Remarks and references to Appendices
HALLENCOURT	14th		Wire to Base for 999 Covers Breech Rifle to complete Units of 31st Div.	
"	15		" " Ordnance VIII Corps. re Disposal of Base Kits.	
"	15		" " Base for 2 Water Tanks for 11th East Lancs to replace 2 Condemned. (Instructions from ADOS VIII Corps Telegram O/13 of 15th.)	
"	15		2800 Blankets received. Repeated to Ord VIII Corps	
"	16		Wire for 1800 Helmets Anti gas for Instructional Purposes.	
			Record and Date of Embarkation of A.O.C. Personnel to AOC Records Etc.	
"	17		Wire to Base for 26 Guns Lewis making 6 guns per Battalion (Authority Ordnance VIII Corps Tel. O/24 of 17th.)	
"	17.		5500 Blankets recd.	
"	18		Wire to Base for 2300 Caps SD to replace Helmets ?? of Units lately arrived.	
"	18		12500 Blankets recd. This completed 2nd Blanket.	
	19		Issue order to Base for Steel Helmets.	
"	19		2390 Blankets retd to Base. 3rd Blanket cancelled by Verbal Arrangement Hd Qrs 31st Div & Ord. VIII Corps.	
"	20		Receipt of 26 Guns Lewis from Base. Reported to VIII Corps.	

2353 Wt. W2544/1454 700,000 5/15 D. D. & L. A.D.S.S./Forms/C. 2118.

Instructions regarding War Diaries and Intelligence Summaries are contained in F. S. Regs., Part II. and the Staff Manual respectively. Title pages will be prepared in manuscript.

WAR DIARY
or
INTELLIGENCE SUMMARY.
(Erase heading not required.)

Army Form C. 2118.

Place	Date	Hour	Summary of Events and Information	Remarks and references to Appendices
Hallencourt	20		3 of A.O.C. personnel cause trouble by being drunk and disorderly (Ptes. Yates, Harker & Rolls) Awarded punishment, and application made at request of G.O.C. to have them immediately exchanged, this was arranged through Ord. VIII Corps. Pt II Orders to A.O.C. Records BEF	
"	24		Wire to Base to suspend issues to railhead until further notice.	
"	25		" " " to proceed with issue of Stores to new railhead	
Bus-les-Artois	27		D.A.D.O.S. & Staff arrive. Very good Office and Dump	
"	28		Wire to Base for 2nd P.H. Helmet (19750) Authority G.H.Q. OC 599/407 of [illegible]	

2353 Wt. W2544/1454 700,000 5/15 D. D. & L. A.D.S.S./Forms/C. 2118.

Instructions regarding War Diaries and Intelligence Summaries are contained in F. S. Regs., Part II. and the Staff Manual respectively. Title pages will be prepared in manuscript.

DADOS 31st Divn

WAR DIARY
or
~~INTELLIGENCE SUMMARY~~.
(Erase heading not required.)

April 1916.

Army Form C. 2118.

Place	Date	Hour	Summary of Events and Information	Remarks and references to Appendices
BUS LES ARTOIS	2nd		Wire to Ordnance VIII Corps for scale of Vermorel Sprayers.	
			10360 P.H. Helmets rec'd. Repeated to ADOS. VIII Corps	
			Ptes Yates, Harper & Rolls AOC left for Base	
	3	4.30pm	Lt R H Johnson AOD reported for duty as DADOS 31st Divn. Arrival of 3 New men from Base Ptes Clark, Mills & Ellsop.	
			Wire to Base for 85 Vermorel Sprayers to complete to 100 per Divn.	
	4		Wire to ADOS VIII Corps re 3900 Steel Helmets in possession. Due on Indent 11873.	
	6		Indent to Base for 1000 Shirts, 1000 Drawers, Socks 1000 prs for Divisl Baths.	
		5.45pm	Lt J McKelly left for Duty with 17 Corps	
	10		Wire to Units to return Winter clothing with exception of 2 Blankets	
	11		Medical Officer's report against advisability of withdrawing Winter Clothing. Wire to Ordnance VIII Corps for instructions	
	12		Wire to Base for 4 Vermorel Sprayers to complete Divn.	
	13		Wire to Base for 20288 PH. Helmets for Divnl Reserve Authority QMG Q.O.S. 317/29/A 48.4.16	
	~~14~~		Repeated to Ordnance VIII Corps	
	14		Wire to Base 2000 Shirts, 3000 Drawers, Socks 3000 & Sacks 200 for Divnl Baths	

Instructions regarding War Diaries and Intelligence Summaries are contained in F. S. Regs., Part II. and the Staff Manual respectively. Title pages will be prepared in manuscript.

WAR DIARY
or
INTELLIGENCE SUMMARY.
(Erase heading not required.)

April 1916 Continued.

Army Form C. 2118.

Place	Date	Hour	Summary of Events and Information	Remarks and references to Appendices
BUS LES ARTOIS	15th		Reported to Ordnance VIII Corps 2895 Helmets SS handed to Railhead by Units	
			do — do — 4834 Steel Helmets in possession of Units	
			Wire to Base for 36 Guns Lewis Authority 4th Army HOB 173 d/ 15th	
			Repeated to Ordnance VIII Corps	
	19		Wire to Base for 2 Guns Vickers to replace Maxims for Lancs Hussars	
			Authority Ord. VIII Corps telegram HG. 126 d/ 19th	
			36 Lewis Guns recd from Base. Informed Ordnance, VIII Corps.	
	20		VIII Corps give permission for retention of Boots Gum Thigh until end of month.	
	22		Receipt of 2 Guns Vickers for Lancs Hussars.	
	25		Guns Maxims 2 returned to Base Tk 142833. These were ~~[illegible]~~ replaced by Vickers	

R H Johnson Lieut
DADOS 31 Divn

2353 Wt. W2544/1454 700,000 5/15 D. D. & L. A.D.S.S. Forms/C 2118.

DADOS
31st Divn

WAR DIARY
or
~~INTELLIGENCE SUMMARY.~~
(Erase heading not required.)

May 1916.

Army Form C. 2118.

Instructions regarding War Diaries and Intelligence Summaries are contained in F. S. Regs., Part II. and the Staff Manual respectively. Title pages will be prepared in manuscript.

Place	Date	Hour	Summary of Events and Information	Remarks and references to Appendices
BUS LES ARTOIS	2		Number of Steel Helmets actually in possession of Units 31 Divn: 8633. Reported to Ord VIII Corps	
	8		2 Water Carriers issued by VIII Corps for trial. Forwarded to 92 Inf Bde	
	9		Report re trial of Water Carrier to Ord VIII Corps	
			Stock and Examination of Spare Parts 18 pr & 4.5 taken by DADOS } Report to ADOS VIII Corps	
	10		Second report re trial of Water Carriers sent to ADOS VIII Corps	
	12		Supply Column request thro' H.Q. 31st Divn for the Ordnance Lorries to be stopped owing to Scarcity of Petrol, finally we were able to retain 2.	
	13		Lanes Hussars & Cyclists Coy cease to be Divnl Troops. Informed ADOS VIII Corps.	
			Report to ADOS VIII Corps re defective Springs in Magazines Lewis Guns	
	14		14369 "P" Anti gas Helmets retd. to ABBEVILLE.	
			Divnl O inserted re retention of 1 blanket per man until June 1st.	
	18		Received from 48 Divn 12 Food Containers.	
	21		Indent to Base for 384 PHG Helmets (Elastic Outside) Authority DDOS. 4th Army HO 3/1/3 d/14inst	

Instructions regarding War Diaries and Intelligence Summaries are contained in F. S. Regs., Part II. and the Staff Manual respectively. Title pages will be prepared in manuscript.

DADOS 31 Div

WAR DIARY
or
INTELLIGENCE SUMMARY.
(Erase heading not required.)

May Continued.

Army Form C. 2118.

Place	Date	Hour	Summary of Events and Information	Remarks and references to Appendices
BUS LES ARTOIS	25.5		Reported change of nomenclature of Batteries (owing to the 171 (How) Bde being divided up ~~Bde~~ Each Bde now consisting of 3 18 pr + 1 4.5 How Bde) to Base & Ord. VIII Corps.	
			Reported 112 Personal Sprayers in possession of Div.	
	29		Steel Helmets in possession 11,666. Reported to Ordnance VIII Corps	
	30		Authority for demand of Gas Helmets for Horses recd. HQ. 1.9.6. O.S.G/6609/495 d/7th	
	31		Total number of Steel Helmets recd to date 15950.	

R H Johnson Lieut
DADOS 31 Divn

2353 Wt. W2544/1454 700,000 5/15 D. D. & L. A.D.S.S. Forms/C. 2118.

D.A.G.

3rd Echelon.

Herewith "War Diary" for June please.

J H Johnson
Lieut
D.A.D.O.S. 31st Div

8/8.

June 1916. 31 DADOS 31st Div June Vol 4

Instructions regarding War Diaries and Intelligence Summaries are contained in F. S. Regs., Part II. and the Staff Manual respectively. Title pages will be prepared in manuscript.

WAR DIARY
or
INTELLIGENCE SUMMARY.
(Erase heading not required.)

Army Form C. 2118.

Place	Date	Hour	Summary of Events and Information	Remarks and references to Appendices
BUSLES ARTOIS	4.6		Lieut N.H. Johnson A.O.D. proceeded on leave. D.A.Q.M.G. 31 Div acted for him.	
	5.6		Wire to Base for 3 3" Trench Mortars for 92/3 T.M. Btys. Trench Mortar Authority VIII Corps	
	7.6		"Bulk" Indent to Base for 20288 Anti Gas Satchels. 2nd Satchel per Officer and man Authority – D.O.S. HC 1/5 H.O. A 3/2/2.	
			Heavy Demands from Units for Paint for camouflage.	
	9.6		Instruction rec'd from VIII Corps to send to I.O.M. Heavy Mobile all Lewis Gun Magazines with defective springs for repair.	
	11.6		30 Covers Sailcloth 30 x 30 demanded from Base for ammunition dumps. (Authority VIII Corps HC 260)	
	15.6		D.A.D.O.S. ret'd from Leave.	
	16.6		5/31 2" T.M. Bty joined Division also Z/23. 2" T.M. Bty.	
	17.6		Bulk demand sent to Base. 520 Regulation 1918 pennants Authority GHQ OB 1656.	
	17.6		14 Trench Carts received from Corps.	
	17.6		12 3" Trench Mortars drawn from Corps. This making 12 Mortars each for 92, 93 + 94 T.M. Btys.	

2353 Wt. W2544/1454 700,000 5/15 D. D. & L. A.D.S.S./Forms/C. 2118.

Instructions regarding War Diaries and Intelligence Summaries are contained in F. S. Regs., Part II. and the Staff Manual respectively. Title pages will be prepared in manuscript.

WAR DIARY
or
INTELLIGENCE SUMMARY.
(Erase heading not required.)

DADOS 31 Div

Army Form C. 2118.

Place	Date	Hour	Summary of Events and Information	Remarks and references to Appendices
BUS LES ARTOIS	19th		Bulk demand to Base for 2,861 Steel Helmets. Authority QMG GHQ QOS/490/A d/ 9th	
	21		Bulk demand to Base for Paint Sand & Brushes for Steel Helmets Authority DOS. OSA/2/6387/3. d/ 4th	
	22		25 Covers Sackcloth demanded from Base for covering dumps.	
	23		No 04860 Pte H E George admitted to hospital	
	23rd		One 3" Mortar received from Base to replace one being sent to Base from 92 T M By with defective block elevating gear	
	25th		Indent to Base for Ordnance QF 4.5" How complete with breech fittings and carriage to replace How 46 burst for D 171 Bde RFA	
	27th		4.5 How No 1160 received from Base for D/171 Bde RFA Damaged gun etc retd to Base	
			Indents for Gun Parts very heavy, particularly Springs running out. J.F.O.	
	28th		Indent to Base for Ordnance QF 4.5 Howitzer complete with breech fittings and carriage to replace How No 93 burst for D/170 Bde RFA	

2353 Wt. W2544/1454 700,000 5/15 D. D. & L. A.D.S.S./Forms/C. 2118.

Instructions regarding War Diaries and Intelligence Summaries are contained in F. S. Regs., Part II. and the Staff Manual respectively. Title page will be prepared in manuscript.

WAR DIARY
or
INTELLIGENCE SUMMARY.
(Erase heading not required.)

Army Form C. 2118.

Place	Date	Hour	Summary of Events and Information	Remarks and references to Appendices
BUS LES ARTOIS	28th		Indent to Base for one 3" Mortar to replace Mortar No 803 Condemned by I.O.M. for 92 T.M. Bty	
	29th		Old QF 4.5 No 1157 received for D/170 Bde RFA	
	30th		Indent to Base for Ordnance QF 4.5 Howitzer complete with breech fittings and Carriage to replace How No 582 burst for D/170 Bde	
	30		Indent to Base for 1664 Carriers Magazine Lewis Gun Authority D.O.S. OS 9916 28/6/16	

[illegible] Lieut
D.A.D.O.S. [illegible] Divn

2353 Wt. W2544/1454 700,000 5/15 D. D. & L. A.D.S.S./Forms/C. 2118.

Confidential Vol ~~4~~ 5

War Diary

of

D.A.D.O.S 3rd Divn

1st July to 31st July

1916

Instructions regarding War Diaries and Intelligence Summaries are contained in F. S. Regs., Part II. and the Staff Manual respectively. Title pages will be prepared in manuscript.

July 1916.

WAR DIARY
or
INTELLIGENCE SUMMARY.
(Erase heading not required.)

DADOS
31st Div

Army Form C. 2118.

Place	Date	Hour	Summary of Events and Information	Remarks and references to Appendices
BUS LES ARTOIS	1.7		Howitzer 4.5 received for D/170 Bde RFA. Damaged Gun & Carriage returned to Base.	
	2.7		Issue of bicycles to Interpreters completed.	
	2.7		Demand sent to Base for 8 Gun Vickers ·303 for 94th Machine Gun Coy	
	2.7		do — do 6 3" Mortars 94th T. M. Bty.	
	2.7		Very heavy demands sent to Base for Gun Parts 18pr & 4.5 for D.A.C.	
	2.7		One Vickers Gun demanded for 92 Machine Gun Coy	
	2.7		One Lewis Gun demanded for 10 East York Regt	
	3.7		Four do — do — for 18 West Yorkshire Regt	
	3.7		Two do do — 16 West Yorks Regt	
	3.7		Six do — do — 15 West Yorkshire Regt	
	3.7		Two do — do — 18 Durham Light Inf	
	3.7		Heavy demands sent to Base for Trench Mortar Parts and Machine Gun parts.	
	3.7		Demand sent to Base for 3 Guns Vickers for 93 Machine Gun Coy	

2353 Wt. W2544/1454 700,000 5/15 D. D. & L. A.D.S.S. Forms/C. 2118.

Instructions regarding War Diaries and Intelligence Summaries are contained in F. S. Regs., Part II. and the Staff Manual respectively. Title pages will be prepared in manuscript.

WAR DIARY
or
INTELLIGENCE SUMMARY.
(Erase heading not required.)

Army Form C. 2118.

Place	Date	Hour	Summary of Events and Information	Remarks and references to Appendices
BUS LES ARTOIS	4.7		Wire to Base to cancel 1 Lewis Gun for 18 West Yorks owing to one being salved	
	4.7		One Lewis Gun rec'd for 10 East Yks.	
	4.7		4 Lewis Guns received for 94 Machine Gun Coy.	
	5.7		6 3" Mortars received for 94 T.M. Bty.	
	5.7		Two Lewis Gun received for 92 Machine Gun Coy	
RIBEAUCOURT	6.7		March. Office and Dump not very satisfactory.	
ST. VENANT	9.7		Good Office. Dump fairly good. Rather a lot of stores owing to units being on Move.	
			Hastened units to indent to complete to Mob. Scale.	
	11.7		Demand for 7 Lewis Guns for 11 East Lancs Regt sent to Base	
	11.7		" " 6 do — 12 York & Lancaster — do —	
	11.7		" " 3 3" T.M. for 92 Bde T M Bty sent to Base	
	11.7		" " 3 2" T.M. for D.T.M.O.	
	11.7		" " 2 Lewis Guns for 14 York & Lancaster sent to Base	
	11.7		All Lewis Guns demanded for 15, 16 & 18 West Yorks and 18 D.L.I. received.	

Instructions regarding War Diaries and Intelligence Summaries are contained in F. S. Regs., Part II. and the Staff Manual respectively. Title pages will be prepared in manuscript.

WAR DIARY
or
INTELLIGENCE SUMMARY.
(Erase heading not required.)

Army Form C. 2118.

Place	Date	Hour	Summary of Events and Information	Remarks and references to Appendices
ST VENANT	14/7		Receipt of 15 Lewis Guns for 94th Bde. & 3 3" Mortars for 92 Bde T.M.Bty.	
	14/7		Lieut B Lankester A.O.D. reported for Duty from Ordnance First Army.	
	14/7		Wire to Base to cancel 3" 2" Mortars for D.T.M.O.	
LESTREM	15/7		Move of Office and Dump	
	16		No 7217 Pte Ibbetson A.O.C. reported for duty from Ordnance Fourth Army.	
	~~17~~ 18			
	19		"Bull" Wire sent to Base for 17730 Helmets P.H.G. Authority 280/2/29(2)&c of 2nd	
	20		Lieut B. Lancaster left today for 2nd Cavalry Division to take duties of D.A.D.O.S.	
	25		Move of Dump on main LOCON-LESTREM road at FOSSE. Wire to Base for Store Tent for Stores A.O.D.	
	30		No 7217 Pte A.R. Ibbetson A.O.C. left for 47 Divn for duty.	
	31		One Vickers Gun demanded for 93 Machine Gun Coy.	

[signature]
DADOS 31 Div.
5-8-16.

2353 Wt. W2544/1454 700,000 5/15 D. D. & L. A.D.S.S. Forms/C. 2118.

Confidential

Vol. ~~VII~~
Vol 6

War Diary
of
D.A.D.O.S. 3rd Divn

Aug. 1916.

Instructions regarding War Diaries and Intelligence Summaries are contained in F. S. Regs., Part II. and the Staff Manual respectively. Title pages will be prepared in manuscript.

D.A.D.O.S. 31st Divn

WAR DIARY or INTELLIGENCE SUMMARY.

(Erase heading not required.)

August 1916.

Army Form C. 2118.

Place	Date	Hour	Summary of Events and Information	Remarks and references to Appendices
LESTREM	1st		Wire to Base for One Ord Q.F. 18 pr to replace Gun No 397 Condemned by IOM for Scoring	
			11 Mortars 3" retd to Base. The establishment of Mortars now being 8 per T.M. Bty 6/71 Bde	
	4		XI Corps Laundry joined Divn from 61st Divn	
			One QF 18 pr Gun recd No 4362 for 6/171 Bde RFA	
			One Vickers Gun No 6423 recd for 93 Machine Gun Coy.	
	9		Wire to Base for one Gun Lewis ·303 to replace one lost for 18 West Yorks Regt	
	11		Indent to Base for 22,000 Dummy Drill Cartridges.	
	12		Lewis Gun recd for 18 West Yorks Regt	
	14		XI Corps Heavy Arty attached to Divn	
	16		Wire to Base for one Gun Vickers to replace No L 3810 Condemned for 92 Machine Gun Coy	
	19		One Vickers Gun No 485 received for 92 Machine Gun Coy.	
	20		Indent to Base for 626 Magazines to complete demand for 64 per Lewis Gun	
	24		491 Coy ASC (XI Corps Heavy Arty) joined Divn for Ordnance Services.	
	25		Trench Mortar Btys renaming - Authority QOS 9/1/48 A.	
	30		Reorganisation of Artillery Brigades.	
	31		150th Siege Bty (6" inch How:) joined Divn	
			J. H. Johnson Lieut DADOS 31 Divn	

2353 Wt. W2544/1454 700,000 5/15 D. D. & L. A.D.S.S./Forms/C. 2118.

Confidential

Volume 7

War Diary.

D. A. D. O. S. 31st Division

September 1916.

Instructions regarding War Diaries and Intelligence Summaries are contained in F. S. Regs., Part II. and the Staff Manual respectively. Title pages will be prepared in manuscript.

WAR DIARY
or
INTELLIGENCE SUMMARY.
(Erase heading not required.)

Army Form C. 2118.

September
Continued

Place	Date	Hour	Summary of Events and Information	Remarks and references to Appendices
BETHUNE	26		Indent to Base for Winter Clothing - (Coats, Drawers & Bands Body) S. 14/235/ 26th	
			Condemned Old QF 18 pr No 367 returned to Base.	
	27		One 2" T.M. received for D.T.M.O. Indent 030/128 dated 21st	
			Wire to Base for 1 3" T.M. for 92 T.M.B to replace one condemned by I.O.M.	
	30		One 3" T.M. No 2242 received from Base for 92 T.M.B	
			Wire to Base for one 18 pr QF (without B.F) to replace No 939 condemned by Sec. I.O.M for Serving for A/170 Bde	
			Wire to Base for 2 3" T.M. condemned by I.O.M. for 92 T.M.B.	

J M Shaw Lieut
DADOS 31 Div

2353 Wt. W2544/1454 700,000 5/15 D. D. & L. A.D.S.S./Forms/C. 2118.

Army Form C. 2118.

Instructions regarding War Diaries and Intelligence Summaries are contained in F. S. Regs., Part II. and the Staff Manual respectively. Title pages will be prepared in manuscript.

DADOS 31st Div.

WAR DIARY or INTELLIGENCE SUMMARY.

(Erase heading not required.)

September 1916.

Place	Date	Hour	Summary of Events and Information	Remarks and references to Appendices
LESTREM	1st		Indent to Base for 19500 Disc Identity No. 1 Green	
	2		Owing to reorganisation of Arty all Indents for Arty Units cancelled	
	3		Demand to Base for 1 2" T.M. for 2/31 TMB to replace one damaged by shell fire. X1 Corps O.S. 32/3.	
	5		— for 4000 prs Boots Gum Thigh Auth. QMG. QOS 4/6/140/A	
	7		— 630 Boots GS (25% Strength of Mounted Men) — do —	
	11		— 15450 Blankets GS (1st Blanket per O.R.) QOS. 5483/4.	
	13		4 – 3.7" TM returned to Base in accordance G.R.O. 532	
	15		Indent for 1 2" TM (2/31) cancelled Parts being salvaged enabling repair by I.O.M.	
	16		2800 Blankets received from Base. {Blankets outstanding from Base cancelled owing to taking over from another Division}	
	17		4110 " "	
BETHUNE	19		Move of Dump & Office to Rue de l'Egalité Bethune	
	21		Indent to Base for one Ord QF 18 pr (without B.F.) for B/169 to replace No. 367	
			Issue of Boots Gum Thigh completed by Base 4008 prs rec'd. Condemned by C.I.O.M. for wear.	
	22		Indent to Base for 1 Lewis Gun to replace No 1365 for 14 Y & L. Condemned	
	23		Division now complete with Steel Helmets – Outstanding demands on base cancelled.	
	24		One Ord. QF 18 pr received from Base for B/169 Bde.	
	25		One Lewis Gun No 15318 received for 14 York & Lancs.	

2353 Wt. W2544/1454 700,000 5/15 D. D. & L. A.D.S.S./Forms/C. 2118.

Confidential. Volume ~~X~~ 8

War Diary.

D. A. D. O. S. 31st Division

October 1916.

Instructions regarding War Diaries and Intelligence Summaries are contained in F. S. Regs., Part II. and the Staff Manual respectively. Title pages will be prepared in manuscript.

WAR DIARY
or
INTELLIGENCE SUMMARY.
(Erase heading not required.)

Army Form C. 2118.

DADOS. 31 Div

October 1916.

Place	Date	Hour	Summary of Events and Information	Remarks and references to Appendices
BETHUNE	1st		26 Lewis Guns rec^d making 10 Lewis Guns per Battalion.	
	3rd		Indent to Base for Box Respirators Small Authority DDOS First Army OS.48/90/58	
	4th		2 3" T.Mortars received for 92 T.M.Bty. Visit of D.D.O.S. First Army.	
	6th		Indent to Base for 20 Covers Sailcloth for Amm^n Dumps.	
			" " " " 365 prs of Boots GS to complete to 25% of Mounted men.	
	7		1 - 18 pr QF. No 4958 rec^d in replacement of Gun No 989 for A/170 Bde RFA.	
MARIEUX	8		Move	
	11		51st Supply Col. attached.	
	11		Bulk indent to Base for Machine Horse Clipping & Clippers Horse.	
	15		Wire to Base for 2600 Steel Helmets to complete for reinforcements	
			" " " " 1 18 pr QF to replace No 443 condemned for wear for B/165 Bde	
AUTHIE	18		Move.	
	19		Indent to Base for 1686 Steel Helmets 1st Supply GRO 1847.	
			" " " " 4000 Capes Mackintosh a Bulk demand for Winter Clothing.	
	20		1 18 pr QF No 5323 (without B.F) received for B/165 Bde to replace No 443.	

Army Form C. 2118.

Instructions regarding War Diaries and Intelligence Summaries are contained in F. S. Regs., Part II. and the Staff Manual respectively. Title pages will be prepared in manuscript.

WAR DIARY
or
INTELLIGENCE SUMMARY.
(Erase heading not required.)

Place	Date	Hour	Summary of Events and Information	Remarks and references to Appendices
AUTHIE	21st		Indent to Base for 300 Braziers Authority Q.O.S. 65/A of 19th	
	23		Move of 51st Div X, Y & Z T.M. Btys to this Div	
			Indent for Overalls for Night Patrols & 3500 Boots [illegible] – G.R.O. 1824	
	24		Indent to Base for 20000 Blankets G.S. (2nd Blanket) Authority Q.O.S. 5639/A d/23rd	
			" " " " 50 Stoves Soyers Authority Reserve Army Q 855/23 d/- 22nd	
	25		Wire for 1 – 2" Trench Mortar for X/31 T.M.B to replace one destroyed,	
			" " 1 – 18 pr QF with Carriage etc for A/170 Bde to replace No 2242 (Shell fire)	
	26		Gun No 4413 despatched to Base in Tk 55129.	
			Move 18th Div X & Y T.M Btys from 51st Div to 31st Div.	
	28		" 19 Div X, Y & Z (2") & W (9.45) Trench Mortar Btys from 19th Div to 31 Div	
	29		Indent to Base for 16 Stoves Beatrice First Supply G.R.O. 1896.	
	31		1150 Blankets, 5755 Undercoats Dur, Boots [illegible] 1086 & 34 Coats Sheepskin lined recd from Base.	

[illegible] Lieut
DADOS 31 Div.

2353 Wt. W2544/1454 700,000 5/15 D. D. & L. A.D.S.S./Forms/C. 2118.

Confidential

Volume XI

Vol 9

War Diary

D. A. D. O. S.

31st Division

November 1916.

DADOS 31st Div.

Instructions regarding War Diaries and Intelligence Summaries are contained in F. S. Regs., Part II. and the Staff Manual respectively. Title pages will be prepared in manuscript.

WAR DIARY
or
INTELLIGENCE SUMMARY.
(Erase heading not required.)

November 1916.

Army Form C. 2118.

Place	Date	Hour	Summary of Events and Information	Remarks and references to Appendices
AUTHIE	2nd		17 Hot Food Containers recd from XIII Corps	
			08860 Pte H.E. George AOC evacuated to No 29 C.C.S.	
	3rd		300 Braziers recd from Base.	
	6th		10 Stoves Soyers do — do.	
	7th		One QF. 18 pr Gun No 610 and Carr No 22565 recd from Base for A/170.	
	9		Wire to Base for One Carr Fd QF 4.5 To replace No C30776 damaged by Hostile Fire for D/165 Bde RFA	
			Indent to Base for 60 Kettles Camp. Authority Fifth Army 035/1.	
			20 Stoves Soyer recd	
	12		Wire to Base for one QF. 18 pr (without B.F.) and Carriage to replace Gun No 194 + Carr No 30717 Condemned by I.O.M. for premature for A/165.	
			One Carr Fd Q.F. No 58837 recd from Base for D/165 Bde.	
	14		Two Lewis Guns withdrawn from 12 KOYLI. Establishment now being 8 Guns per Pioneer Battalion. Authority Fifth Army 0/2/3/1	
			Reinforcement 010439 Pte Fielding AOC relief for Pte George arrives	
			Wire to Base for One Lewis Gun to replace one destroyed by Shell Fire for 15 West Yorks Regt	

A5834 Wt. W4973/M687 750,000 8/16 D. D. & L. Ltd. Forms/C.2118/13.

Instructions regarding War Diaries and Intelligence Summaries are contained in F. S. Regs., Part II. and the Staff Manual respectively. Title pages will be prepared in manuscript.

WAR DIARY
or
INTELLIGENCE SUMMARY.
(Erase heading not required.)

Army Form C. 2118.

Place	Date	Hour	Summary of Events and Information	Remarks and references to Appendices
AUTHIE	15th		The 2 Lewis Guns withdrawn from 12 KOYLI reissued to 3rd Divn.	
			Six Stoves Soyers recd.	
	16th		Wire to Base for 1 Lewis Gun to replace one lost in action for 10 E. Yks Regt (This Indent was cancelled later on instructions from XIII Corps. Provision being made locally)	
			18th, 19th & 51st T M Btys rejoin their Divisions.	
	17		517th (How) Bty, R.F.A attached to Divn. for administration.	
			Under arrangements from XIII Corps, 17 and 2 Lewis Guns were drawn from the 3rd & 32nd Divisions respectively to replace our losses in action on 13 inst. Issues as follows:– 8 to 12th E. Yks ; 8 to 13th East Yks and one each to 10 E. Yks, 11 E. Yks & 11 E. Lancs.	
			Total number of 2nd Blanket received to date 8200.	
	18		Large demands for Equipment etc to complete to Mob. Scale, all possible use was made of Salvage dump which assisted greatly in the supply of accoutrements etc.	
			One QF 18 pr No 5787 + Carr No 63689, One QF 18 pr No 5835 and One Lewis Gun No 8168 recd and issued to A/165, B/170 & 15 W Yks respectively.	

A5834 Wt. W4973/M687 750,000 8/16 D. D. & L. Ltd. Forms/C.2118/13.

Instructions regarding War Diaries and Intelligence Summaries are contained in F. S. Regs., Part II. and the Staff Manual respectively. Title pages will be prepared in manuscript.

WAR DIARY
or
INTELLIGENCE SUMMARY.
(Erase heading not required.)

Army Form C. 2118.

Place	Date	Hour	Summary of Events and Information	Remarks and references to Appendices
AUTHIE.	19th		Condemned Gun & Carr in Tk 11110 & One Gun QF 18 pr in Tk 21374 despatched to Base.	
	21st		Pte George returns to duty. To be retained with DADOS vide instructions from Fifth Army.	
			Two Men A.O.C. arrive to give instructions for repair of Gum Boots.	
	22nd		D.A.D.O.S. proceeded on leave.	
			Indent to Corps for 400 Bags Ration Special Fifth Army R.O. 236.	
			Wire to Base for one Carr Fd QF 4.5 to replace No C21984 damaged by hostile fire for D/170 Bde.	
			— do — do One QF 18 pr (without B.M) to replace No 1271. Condemned for scoring for A/169 Bde.	
	24th		3000 Blankets recd making total to date 11200.	
	25th		Wire to Base for one 3" Stokes Mortar to replace one condemned by I.O.M for 93 Trench Mortar Btn.	
	26th		8260 Blankets and 6800 Jerkins Leather recd.	
	28th		One Carr Fd Q.F. 4.5 No 85773 and One Q.F. 18 pr (without B.M) No 5140 received and issued to D/170 and A/169 Bde.	
	29		Condemned QF 18 pr No 1271 and Carr Q.F. 4.5 No 22441 despatched to Base in Tk 54666.	
	30th		MOVE 82nd Fd Coy R.E. from 19th Divn to this Divn for administration.	H A Johnson [illegible] DADOS 31 Div

A5834 Wt. W4973/M687 750,000 8/16 D. D. & L. Ltd. Forms/C.2118/13.

Confidential   Volume XII

Vol 10

War Diary

D. A. D. O. S.   31st. Division

December 1916

Instructions regarding War Diaries and Intelligence Summaries are contained in F. S. Regs., Part II. and the Staff Manual respectively. Title pages will be prepared in manuscript.

December 1916

WAR DIARY
or
INTELLIGENCE SUMMARY.
(Erase heading not required.)

D.A.D.O.S. 31st Division

Army Form C. 2118.

Place	Date	Hour	Summary of Events and Information	Remarks and references to Appendices
AUTHIE	8th		Demand for 2nd Blanket now complete.	
	9		Division now complete with Stove Soyers	
	10		MOVE Essex Yeomanry Coy of 8 Cav Pioneer Bn from 4th to 31st Divn	
	11		4640 Small Box Respirators received	
	13		Indent to Base for 3000 Cartridge S.A. Dummy Authority DOS OSB 2/1255/9	
	14		6200 Small Box Respirators received	
			MOVE 5th Supply Col from 51st Divn to 31st Divn	
	15		3100 Small Box Respirators received	
	18		Wire to Base for One 18 pr QF and Carriage to replace Gun No 331 & Carr. No C12351 rendered unserviceable by premature for C/165 Bde RFA	
	20		Indent to Base for 660 Blankets GS Authority OB 1451 d/ 9th	
	21		Wire to Base for One 18 pr QF & Carriage to replace Gun No 1488 & Carr No C2429 rendered unserviceable by premature for C/165 Bde RFA	
	22		Gun No 3071 & Carr No 38786 received for C/165 Bde RFA	
	24		MOVE 82 Fd Coy to 19th Divn from 31st Divn	
	26		MOVE 91 Fd Coy from 19 Divn to 31st Divn	

2353 Wt. W2544/1454 700,000 5/15 D. D. & L. A.D.S.S. Forms/C. 2118.

Instructions regarding War Diaries and Intelligence Summaries are contained in F. S. Regs., Part II. and the Staff Manual respectively. Title pages will be prepared in manuscript.

WAR DIARY
or
INTELLIGENCE SUMMARY.
(Erase heading not required.)

Army Form C. 2118.

Place	Date	Hour	Summary of Events and Information	Remarks and references to Appendices
AUTHIE	25th		2000 Small Box Respirators recd. This completes demand.	
	26th		Wire to Base for one 18 pr QF & Carriage to replace No 1853 and C 33223 rendered unserviceable by premature for A/165 Bde RFA	
			Gun No 3717 and Carriage No 64407 received for C/165 Bde RFA	
	28th		MOVE 6th Cav Bde Pioneer Coy from 3 Cavalry Divn to 31 Div	
	30		Gun No 170 and Carriage No C64406 received for A/165 Bde RFA	

J H Johnson Captain
DADOS 31 Div.

Confidential

Volume ~~XIII~~

Vol XI

War Diary

D. A. D. O. S. 31st Division

January 1917

Instructions regarding War Diaries and Intelligence Summaries are contained in F. S. Regs., Part II. and the Staff Manual respectively. Title pages will be prepared in manuscript.

D.A.D.O.S. 31st Div.

WAR DIARY
or
INTELLIGENCE SUMMARY.
(Erase heading not required.)

January 1917.

Army Form C. 2118.

Place	Date	Hour	Summary of Events and Information	Remarks and references to Appendices
AUTHIE	1st		Indent to Base for 200 Body Shields & Necklets - Authority Fifth Army 0/1/41 d/29th	
			24 Lewis Guns received from Base this making 12 guns per Battalion.	
			One 2" inch T.M. received for X/31 T.M. Bty (Demanded 24th October '16.)	
			Indent to Base for One Lewis Gun for Instructional Purposes - Authority 1538/44 (QA3) d/22nd	
	2		" " " " 370 Ayrton Flapper Fans to complete Divn - Authority Q.O.S/317/27/A d/26th	
	4		Wire to Base for One Gun Vickers to replace one condemned by Divnl Armourers for 92 M.G. Coy	
	5		One Lewis Gun received for School of Instruction	
	9		Wire to Base for One Gun Vickers to replace one condemned by Divnl Armourers for 93 M.G. Coy.	
BEAUVAL	11		MOVE	
	12		Vickers Guns Nos 2046 & 1097 received and issued to 92 & 93 Machine Gun Coy respectively.	
	13		Move of Pte L.E. Fitzpatrick to XIII Corps. Pte H Eldridge from XIII Corps to 31st Divn	
			Wire to Base for One QF 18 pr without BM to replace No 1273 condemned for scoring for A/169 Bde	
			" " " One QF 18 pr Carriage to replace No C/42135 rendered unserviceable by hostile fire for B/169 Bde RFA	
			" " " One Gun Vickers to replace one destroyed by shell fire for 94 M.G. Coy	
	16		One QF 18 pr No 274, Carr No 30742 and Gun Vickers No 5100 received and issued to A/169, B/169 & 94 Machine Gun Coy respectively.	

2353 Wt. W2544/1454 700,000 5/15 D. D. & L. A.D.S.S./Forms/C. 2118.

Army Form C. 2118.

Instructions regarding War Diaries and Intelligence Summaries are contained in F. S. Regs., Part II. and the Staff Manual respectively. Title pages will be prepared in manuscript.

WAR DIARY
or
INTELLIGENCE SUMMARY.

(Erase heading not required.)

Place	Date	Hour	Summary of Events and Information	Remarks and references to Appendices
BERNAVILLE	22		MOVE	
			Wire to Base for One QF 18 pr to replace No 610 condemned for scoring for	
	25		One QF 18 pr No 3319 received & issued to A/170 Bde RFA. (A/170 Bde RFA)	

H 2/17

J. H. Johnson Capt
DADOS. 31 Div

Confidential

Volume XIV.

Vol 12

War Diary.

D.A.D.O.S. 31st Division

February 1917.

D.A.D.O.S. 31st Divn

Instructions regarding War Diaries and Intelligence Summaries are contained in F. S. Regs., Part II. and the Staff Manual respectively. Title pages will be prepared in manuscript.

WAR DIARY or INTELLIGENCE SUMMARY.

(Erase heading not required.)

February 1917

Army Form C. 2118.

Place	Date	Hour	Summary of Events and Information	Remarks and references to Appendices
BERNAVILLE	1st		One Vickers Gun received from Base for 94th Machine Gun Coy.	
	2nd		24 Lewis Guns received from Base. Each Battalion now in possession of 14 Lewis Guns.	
	4th		Large consignments of Stores being received from Base, in satisfaction of Units demands to complete to Mobn Scale.	
	6th		Paillasses being issued.	
	7th		Arrangements completed for "Thaw Precautions", Store Tent pitched at CANAPLES.	
	7th		Return to Ordl. XIII Corps stated "Average number of Boots repaired in Divn monthly is 6608".	
	13th		S/Condr Freeman & Pte Johnson A.O.C. proceed to 18th Divn to assist in administration of 31st Divnl Artiy & 23rd Army Fd Artiy Bde.	
	14th		Wire to Base to suspend issues owing to impending move. Thaw Precautions.	
	18th		Two truck received, but owing to move Units unable to draw from Railhead.	
AUTHIE	21st		Move - Good Office - great difficulty in finding suitable dump.	
	22nd		Stores reconsigned from CANAPLES. Take over II Corps Troops Store Tent at BELLE EGLISE	

2353 Wt. W2544/1454 700,000 5/15 D. D. & L. A.D.S.S./Forms/C. 2118.

Instructions regarding War Diaries and Intelligence Summaries are contained in F. S. Regs., Part II. and the Staff Manual respectively. Title pages will be prepared in manuscript.

WAR DIARY
or
INTELLIGENCE SUMMARY.
(Erase heading not required.)

Army Form C. 2118.

Place	Date	Hour	Summary of Events and Information	Remarks and references to Appendices
AUTHIE	23rd		Wire to 18th Divn for our representatives to return as the Divnl Arty have rejoined Divn	
	25th		Complaints from R.T.O. & R.O.O BELLE EGLISE re non clearance of trucks at Railhead. Transport not available.	
	27th		Instructions to Bde W.O's at BERNAVILLE to move all Stores etc by rail from CANDAS to BELLE EGLISE.	
	28th		Wire to Base for 2 Guns Vickers to replace 2 destroyed by Shell fire for 93 Machine Gun Coy.	

10/3/17

J H Johnson Capt
DADOS 31 Divn

2353 Wt. W2544/1454 700,000 5/15 D. D. & L. A.D.S.S./Forms/C. 2118.

Confidential.

Volume XV

Vol 13

War Diary.

D.A.D.O.S.

31st. Division.

March 1917.

Instructions regarding War Diaries and Intelligence Summaries are contained in F. S. Regs., Part II. and the Staff Manual respectively. Title pages will be prepared in manuscript.

WAR DIARY
or
INTELLIGENCE SUMMARY.
(Erase heading not required.)

D.A.D.O.S. 31st Divn

Army Form C. 2118.

March 1917.

Place	Date	Hour	Summary of Events and Information	Remarks and references to Appendices
AUTHIE	1st		Wire to Base "Owing to Transport Difficulties can only accept Urgent Stores"	
			Arrival of Stores and A.O.C. personnel from BERNAVILLE	
	2nd		Urgent Demands from Arty for Buffer Oil	
	3		Change of Railhead – Stores & Stone Tent reconsigned from Belle Eglise to Beaussart	
			Packsaddlery Drawn from Vth Corps Troops.	
	4		Wire to Base for 2 Lewis Guns to replace 2 lost for 16th West Yorks Regt	
COUIN	5		Move Good Office and Dump.	
	6		Two Vickers Guns received and issued to 93 Machine Gun Coy	
	7		Owing to lack of Transport cannot move Stores from AUTHIE	
	8		Road Precautions off & Lorries used in lieu of Horse Transport.	
	9		Divl Gum Boot Repair Shop formed as distinct from Gum Boot Store	
	10		Wire to Base "Stores can now be accepted"	
			Two Lewis Guns received and issued to 16 West Yorks Regt.	
	12		Wire to Base for One Lewis Gun to replace one lost for 12 York & Lancs	
	14		Urgent Demand for Boots. Special Wire sent to Base.	
			Wire to Base for One Lewis Gun to replace one lost for 11th East Lancs.	
			Wire to Base for One Q.F. How 4·5 with Carriage to replace No 517 burst for D/170 Bde RFA	

Army Form C. 2118.

WAR DIARY
or
INTELLIGENCE SUMMARY.
(Erase heading not required.)

Instructions regarding War Diaries and Intelligence Summaries are contained in F. S. Regs., Part II. and the Staff Manual respectively. Title pages will be prepared in manuscript.

Place	Date	Hour	Summary of Events and Information	Remarks and references to Appendices
COUIN	15th		Wired to Base for One Lewis Gun to replace one lost for 14 York & Lancs.	
	16th		Wired to Base for One QF 18 pr to replace one damaged by Hostile fire for C/165 Bde RFA	
			Lewis Gun received for 12 York & Lancs	
	17th		Issue of all Stores suspended from Base owing to impending move.	
			Report sent to Corps of 11 Lewis Gun Handcarts returned by Units to Railhead.	
	19th		Two Lewis Guns received. One for 11 East Lancs & 14 York & Lancs respectively.	
	20th		24 Lewis Guns Received. This issue completing each Battalion to 16 Guns.	
ST VENANT	21st		Move. 31 Division Artillery to 1st Canadian Division.	
	24th		One QF How 4.5 received from Base for D/170 Bde RFA	
	26th		One QF 18 pr received from Base for C/165 Bde RFA	
	27th		Ordnance Lorries exchanged from 5th to 31st Supply Column.	
	28th		Orders published for Units to examine Mob. Equipment and Indent to replace deficiencies	
	30th		Large demands for Paint. G.O.C. desires all Wagons & Vehicles to be repainted immediately.	
	30th		A.D.O.S. XIII Corps sanctions return of Undercoats Fur & Leather Jerkins	

J M Johnson Capt
DADOS. 31 Div.

2353 Wt. W2544/1454 700,000 5/15 D. D. & L. A.D.S.S./Forms/C 2118.

Confidential

Volume XVI

Vol 14

War Diary

D.A.D.O.S. 31st Division

April 1917

D.A.D.O.S.
31st Div.

Army Form C. 2118.

WAR DIARY
or
INTELLIGENCE SUMMARY.
(Erase heading not required.)

April 1917

Instructions regarding War Diaries and Intelligence Summaries are contained in F. S. Regs., Part II. and the Staff Manual respectively. Title pages will be prepared in manuscript.

Place	Date	Hour	Summary of Events and Information	Remarks and references to Appendices
ST VENANT	2nd		Additional Limber for Lewis Guns hastened from Base:	
	3rd		Indent to Base for 18970 Goggles Anti Gas Rubber Sponge.	
	4th		Demand to Base for 10000 prs Socks as a Divnl Reserve at Laundry.	
		6pm	Opening of First Army Ord: Gun Park.	
	5th		Move of 223 Fd Coy RE to 1st Canadian Divn for Ord: Administration.	
	7th		Wire to Ord. 63 Divn re taking over Dump.	
BETHUNE	9th		Move. Good Office & Storage accommodation.	
	10th		Indent to Base for Tabs & Buttons for alteration of Greatcoats.	
	14th		Withdrawal of 1st Blanket.	
	17th		W.O. & 2 men sent to 2nd Divn to administer 31st Divnl Arty.	
	18th		Pails and Rope received for use with Water Tank carts.	
BRUAY.	19th		Move	

Instructions regarding War Diaries and Intelligence Summaries are contained in F. S. Regs., Part II. and the Staff Manual respectively. Title pages will be prepared in manuscript.

WAR DIARY
or
INTELLIGENCE SUMMARY.
(Erase heading not required.)

Army Form C. 2118.

Place	Date	Hour	Summary of Events and Information	Remarks and references to Appendices
BRUAY	20th		Conference at XIII Corps re difficulties experienced at Gun Park	
	24th		Wire to Gun Park for one Vickers to replace one destroyed by hostile fire for 93 Machine Gun Coy	
HERIPRE	25th		Move.	
	26th		Move of 18 D.L.I. to 63 Divn for Ord administration	
	27th		One Vickers Gun received and issued for 93 Machine Gun Coy	
			Wire to Gun Park for One Vickers to replace one condemned for 93 Machine Gun Coy	
	28th		Storage accommodation required for Salvage and underclothing.	
	29th		Petrol Cans brought from Bruay.	
	30th		One Vickers Gun received and issued to 93 Machine Gun Coy.	
	30th		MOVE	
MARŒUIL				
			4/5/17	
			H. K. Johnson Capt DADOS 31 Divn	

2353 Wt. W2544/1454 700,000 5/15 D. D. & L. A.D.S.S./Forms/C. 2118.

Confidential

Volume XVII

Vol 15

War Diary.

D.A.D.O.S. 31st. Division

May 1917.

Instructions regarding War Diaries and Intelligence Summaries are contained in F. S. Regs., Part II. and the Staff Manual respectively. Title pages will be prepared in manuscript.

May 1917.

WAR DIARY
or
INTELLIGENCE SUMMARY.
(Erase heading not required.)

D.A.D.O.S. 31st Divn

Army Form C. 2118.

Place	Date	Hour	Summary of Events and Information	Remarks and references to Appendices
MAROEUIL	1/5/17		Demand recd from C/311 A.F.A. Bde for 3 Carriages QF 18 pr to replace 3 damaged by Hostile Fire	
	2		" " " C/311 " " " 2 QF 18 pr to replace 2 which were unable to be moved by I.O.M. from damaged carriages.	
			MOVE of 31st Divnl Arty to 31st Divn from 2nd Divn. A dump being establishment for their convenience at ARRAS.	
	3		36 Lewis Guns & 5 Vickers drawn from Gun Park for issue to 15, 18 West Yks Regt 18 Durham L Inf and 93 Machine Gun Coy.	
			Wire to Base for 2 - 3" Stokes Trench Mortars to replace 2 lost in action by 93 T.M. Bty.	
			MOVE to 31st Divn from 63 Divn 86 & 311 Army Fd Arty Bdes.	
	4		Demand recd from C/165 R.F.A. for 1 QF 18 pr & Carriage to replace others damaged by Hostile Fire	
			MOVE 9th Labour Coy Devon Regt & 12 Labour Coy RW Surrey Regt from XIII Corps Troops to 31st Divn	
			Wire to Gun Park for 28 Lewis Guns to replace losses by 10, 11 & 12 East Yks Regt	
	5		Demand recd from D/170 Bde for 1 QF 4.5 how to replace one damaged by Hostile Fire	
			" " " C/86 A.F.A. Bde for 1 Wagon Ammn to replace one condemned.	
			Wire to Base to cancel demand for 2 3" Stokes 6 being salvaged by 93 T.M. Bty.	
	6		2 QF 18 pr recd for C/311 A.F.A. Bde & 1 QF 18 pr recd for C/165 R.F.A.	

2353 Wt. W2544/1454 700,000 5/15 D. D. & L. A.D.S.S./Forms/C. 2118.

Instructions regarding War Diaries and Intelligence Summaries are contained in F. S. Regs., Part II. and the Staff Manual respectively. Title pages will be prepared in manuscript.

WAR DIARY
or
INTELLIGENCE SUMMARY.
(Erase heading not required.)

Army Form C. 2118.

Place	Date	Hour	Summary of Events and Information	Remarks and references to Appendices
	7/5		The Lewis & Vickers Guns rec^d from Gun Park examined by Divisl Armourers. Issues made of 13 to 15 W Yks, 8 to 18 W Yks, 9 to 16 W Yks & 1 to 14 York & Lancs also 4 Vickers issued to 93 Machine Gun Co from Guns rec^d on the 3rd inst, other guns being salved meanwhile by Units	
			2 Carriages QF 18 pr available at Gun Pk for C/311 A.F.A. Bde.	
			MOVE to 31st Div^n from XIII Corps Troops of 21st Labour Coy	
	8^5		Wire to Base for 10 Tarpaulins for Amm^n Dumps	
			1 Vickers Gun issued to 94 Machine Gun Co to replace one damaged.	
	9^5		Demand rec^d from 311 Army F.A. Bde Amm^n Col for 1 Limber QF 18 pr to replace one condemned	
	10		28 Lewis Guns rec^d, and issues made of 8 to 10 E Yks, 12 to 12 E Yks & 8 to 11 E Yks	
			MOVE to 31st Div^n from HOME 15 Labour Coy Lincoln Regt.	
			Third carriage available at Gun Park for C/311 A.F.A. Bde.	
	11		One Limber QF 18 pr & 1 Wagon Amm^n rec^d for 311 Amm^n Col & C/165 respectively	
	12		1 Lewis Gun issued to 15 W^est Yks	
			Two 2" Medium Trench Mortars surplus to establishment ret^d to Base.	
	13		One QF 4.5 how rec^d for D/170 Bde. Demand sent to Gun Park for 1 Wagon Amm^n QF 18 pr for 72 A.F. Bde Amm^n Col	

2353 Wt. W2544/1454 700,000 5/15 D. D. & L. A.D.S.S./Forms/C. 2118.

Instructions regarding War Diaries and Intelligence Summaries are contained in F. S. Regs., Part II. and the Staff Manual respectively. Title pages will be prepared in manuscript.

WAR DIARY
or
INTELLIGENCE SUMMARY.
(Erase heading not required.)

Army Form C. 2118.

Place	Date	Hour	Summary of Events and Information	Remarks and references to Appendices
	14th		One QF 4.5 how rec'd for D/311 A.F.A Bde	
			MOVE to 31st Div. of 7/2 Army F.A Bde & 4th Labour Coy Devon Regt from 5th Div & XVIII Corps Troops respectively.	
			Demand rec'd from A/72 A.F.A Bde for 1 QF 18 pr to replace one condemned for scoring	
			Four 3" Stokes Mortars salvaged by 93 T.M. Bty rec'd to Base.	
	15th		1500 Anti Gas Respirators for horses rec'd from XIII Corps Troops.	
			Demands rec'd from H.Q. 31st D.A.C. & No 2 Sec D.A.C. for 1 Limber QF 18 pr to replace condemned	
			Additional Limbered Wagon G.S. for carriage of Lewis Gun Equipment received	
	16		3 Lewis Guns issued to 12 Y&Lancs to replace 3 condemned.	
	1		All sections of 176 Tunnelling Coy now administered by 31st Div	
			One 18 pr QF rec'd for A/72 A.F.A. Bde	
	17		19th Labour Coy R.W. Surrey Regt join Div from XVII Corps Troops.	
			1 Limber QF 18 pr rec'd for 311 Army F.A Bde	
	19		Demand rec'd from A/165 Bde for 1 QF 18 pr to replace one condemned for scoring	
			1 Wagon Amm QF 18 pr rec'd for C/86 A.F.A Bde	
			Demand rec'd from D/165 Bde for 1 QF 18 pr to replace one damaged by Hostile Fire	

Instructions regarding War Diaries and Intelligence Summaries are contained in F. S. Regs., Part II. and the Staff Manual respectively. Title pages will be prepared in manuscript.

WAR DIARY
or
INTELLIGENCE SUMMARY.
(Erase heading not required.)

Army Form C. 2118.

Place	Date	Hour	Summary of Events and Information	Remarks and references to Appendices
	20th		Up to this period 29 Lewis Guns & 2 Vickers have been made up (from Guns and Gun Parts salvaged by Units) in Divl Armourers Shop, which with the exception of 6 Lewis Guns sent to Gun Park were reissued to replace losses etc.	
			MOVE 72 & 86 Army F.A. Bdes from 31st Divn to X Corps Troops	
			" 311 Army F A Bde from 31st Divn to 1st New Zealand Divn	
	21st		4 Additional Armourers join Divl Armourers Shop	
	22		Store Tent pitched for receiving Old Service Dress	
	23		Wagon limber QF 18 pr recd for 31st D.A.C.	
	24		Demand recd from B/165 for 1 QF 18 pr to replace one condemned for scoring	
	25		Instructions issued for return of 2nd Blanket.	
			Demand recd from B/170 for 1 QF 18 pr to replace one condemned for scoring	
			Wire to Gun Park for 1 Lewis for 14 York & Lancs.	
	26		One QF 4.5 & carr recd for D/165 Bde & 1 QF 18 pr for A/165 Bde	
			Demand recd from A/165 for 2 QF 18 pr to replace two condemned for scoring	
	27		30 Party Employment Coy join Divn from Base	
			One Lewis Gun recd for 14 York & Lancs.	

2353 Wt. W2544/1454 700,000 5/15 D. D. & L. A.D.S.S./Forms/C. 2118.

Instructions regarding War Diaries and Intelligence Summaries are contained in F. S. Regs., Part II. and the Staff Manual respectively. Title pages will be prepared in manuscript.

WAR DIARY
or
INTELLIGENCE SUMMARY.
(Erase heading not required.)

Army Form C. 2118.

Place	Date	Hour	Summary of Events and Information	Remarks and references to Appendices
	29th		One Q.F. 18 pr recd for B/170 RFA & 1 QF 18 pr for B/165 Bde RFA	
			MOVE 47 Labour Coy to 31st Divn from 63 Div	
	30th		6 men from 30th Employment Coy join Ordnance Detatchment to replace 6 fatigue men.	
			1/6/17	
			J H Johnson Capt DADOS. 31st Div	

Confidential

Volume XVIII

Vol 16

War Diary.

D.A.D.O.S. 31st Division

June 1917

June 1917

WAR DIARY
or
INTELLIGENCE SUMMARY.
(Erase heading not required.)

Army Form C. 2118.

D.A.D.O.S.
31st Divn

Instructions regarding War Diaries and Intelligence Summaries are contained in F. S. Regs., Part II. and the Staff Manual respectively. Title pages will be prepared in manuscript.

Place	Date	Hour	Summary of Events and Information	Remarks and references to Appendices
MAROEUIL	1st		Wire to Base for one Watercart to replace one condemned for 12 E Yorks Regt	
	2		D.A.D.O.S. proceeded on leave.	
			Two QF 18 prs received for A/165 R.F.A. to replace Nos 170 & 3322	
	4		Large Demands for paint received from Units.	
	6		Demand recd from A/165 for one Q.F 4.5 How to replace gun number unknown despatched to Base.	
	7		Demand recd from C/165 for one QF 18 pr to replace 4439 condemned for scoring.	
			100 Yukon Pack received from XIII Corps.	
			Correspondence with Q.M.G. re Howitzer demanded for A/165 Bde.	
	8		Demand recd from A/170 Bde for one 18 pr to replace V.S.M./2823 condemned for scoring.	
	9		Demand recd from B/170 Bde for two 18 pr's to replace EOC/1953 & 2987 both condemned for scoring.	
	9		Indent to Base for 3 German Machine Guns for instructional purposes to complete Divn to scale (Authority Q.M.G 28/2 (Q.A.3) of 15th	

Instructions regarding War Diaries and Intelligence Summaries are contained in F. S. Regs., Part II. and the Staff Manual respectively. Title pages will be prepared in manuscript.

WAR DIARY
or
INTELLIGENCE SUMMARY.
(Erase heading not required.)

Army Form C. 2118.

Place	Date	Hour	Summary of Events and Information	Remarks and references to Appendices
ST. CATHERINE	10th		MOVE.	
	11		Report to Corps stating that all Large Box Respirators have been retd. to Base	
			99 Tins (new pattern) for carrying water drawn from XIII Corps.	
	13		Demand received from C/170 Bde for one 18 pr to replace No. E.O.C/1952 condemned for scoring.	
			D.A.D.O.S. returns from leave.	
	14		MOVE 176 Tunnelling Coy from 63rd Divn to 31st Divn.	
	16		Indent to Base for Flapper Fans to complete Divn to scale.	
	17		Wire to Base cancelling 4.5 howitzer demanded for A/165 Bde, one being available with D.O.M. 63rd Divn	
	18		MOVE 120 Labour Coy from 31st Divn to 63rd Divn	
	19		Demand recd from C/170 Bde for one 18 pr to replace VSM/2348 condemned for scoring.	
			" " " A/165 Bde for one 18 pr to replace E.O.C. 4362 condemned for scoring.	
			" " " 92 Machine Gun Coy for one Guns Vickers to replace one condemned.	
	21		One Vickers Gun recd and issued to 92 Machine Gun Coy.	
			90 Sprayers for Manure heaps received from Base.	

A5834 Wt. W4973/M687 750,000 8/16 D. D. & L. Ltd. Forms/C.2118/13.

Instructions regarding War Diaries and Intelligence Summaries are contained in F. S. Regs., Part II. and the Staff Manual respectively. Title pages will be prepared in manuscript.

WAR DIARY
or
INTELLIGENCE SUMMARY.
(Erase heading not required.)

Army Form C. 2118.

Place	Date	Hour	Summary of Events and Information	Remarks and references to Appendices
ST. CATHERINE	24th		Indent to Gun Park for 4 Breech Mechanisms 18 pr under Authority of W.O. letter A2/1917/660 dated 15/5/17.	
	"		Demand rec^d from C/140 for one 18 pr to replace 3814 withdrawn }	
			" " " A/140 " " 18 pr " " 4958 " }	
	25th		Demand rec^d from A/140 for one QF 18 pr to replace No 3309 condemned for scoring. Authority Q.M.G 3/21 (Q.B.3)	
	26		MOVE 108 Bty 23 Bde from 46 Div to 31st Div^n.	
	29		Demand rec^d from A/140 for one QF 18 pr to replace V.S.M 2111 condemned for scoring.	
			Indent to Base for 16 Lucas Daylight Sig Lamps to complete Arty to scale.	
			Demand rec^d from 93 Machine Gun Co for one Vickers to replace one condemned.	
	30		Reported 9 Chaff Cutters received from Base.	
			Demand rec^d from C/140 for one 18 pr to replace No E.O.C/3233 condemned for scoring.	
			J. H. [illegible] Capt. DADOS 31 Div.	

5/7/17

A5834 Wt. W4973/M687 750,000 8/16 D. D. & L. Ltd. Forms/C.2118/13.

Confidential

Volume XIX

Vol 17

War Diary

D. A. D. O. S. 31st Division

July 1917.

Instructions regarding War Diaries and Intelligence Summaries are contained in F. S. Regs., Part II. and the Staff Manual respectively. Title pages will be prepared in manuscript.

DADOS
31 Division

WAR DIARY
or
~~INTELLIGENCE SUMMARY.~~
(Erase heading not required.)

July 1917.

Army Form C. 2118.

Place	Date	Hour	Summary of Events and Information	Remarks and references to Appendices
ST CATHERINE	1		Received one Vickers Gun to replace L 4694 for 93 Machine Gun Coy. Issued.	
			Indent for one Vickers Gun for 92 Machine Gun Coy to replace L2673 condemned by 31 Divisional Armourer.	
			Demand received from B/165 for one 18 pr to replace 11806 condemned for scoring.	
	2		MOVES:- 12 K.O.Y.L.I. Infantry (Pioneers) to 39th Division	
			C/165 Bde R.F.A. to First Army Troops for Ordnance Administration (except Gun Stores)	
MARCOEUIL	4		MOVE	
	6		MOVES:- 120 Labour Coy from 63rd Division	
			108 Battery 23 Army Field Artillery Bde. to 4th Division	
	8		Demand received from A/165 Bde R.F.A. for one 18 pdr to replace 14044 condemned for scoring.	
	9		Four part worn Breech Mechanisms despatched to Base. Four new issued	
	10		Received and issued one Vickers Gun to 92 Machine Gun Coy.	
			Demand received from 92 Machine Gun Coy for one Vickers Gun to replace L 5884 condemned.	
			Demand for Armbands Billet Warden - 40.	

A5834 Wt. W4973/M687 750,000 8/16 D. D. & L. Ltd. Forms/C.2118/13.

Instructions regarding War Diaries and Intelligence Summaries are contained in F. S. Regs., Part II. and the Staff Manual respectively. Title pages will be prepared in manuscript.

DADOS. 31 Divn

WAR DIARY
or
~~INTELLIGENCE SUMMARY.~~
(Erase heading not required.)

July 1917.

Army Form C. 2118.

Place	Date	Hour	Summary of Events and Information	Remarks and references to Appendices
MARŒUIL	11		Received and issued one Vickers Gun to 92 Machine Gun Coy.	
			Wire to Base to suspend issues until further notice	
			Demand received from 92 Trench Mortar Batty for one Mounting to replace condemned	
	12		MOVE. Lieut E.G. DAVIES, A.O.D. from 5th Division in continuance of instruction in the duties of D.A.D.O.S.	
			Wire to Base to resume issues	
			Indent to Base for 14000 Covers for Steel Helmets.	
	13		MOVE. 42 Chinese Labour Coy. from L. of C.	
	14		MOVE Y/31 Trench Mortar Batty (2" Medium) to 57th Division	
			Large Demand for Paint received from Units.	
	15		MOVE. 174 Labour Coy. to XIV Corps Troops.	
			C/165 Bde R.F.A. from First Army Troops.	
			Demand received from 94 Trench Mortar Batty for one Stand II to replace condemned Fastener. One Mounting for 92 Trench Mortar Batty demanded on the 11th.	
	16		Demand for 180 Stencil Brushes submitted, for repainting Divisional Sign.	

Instructions regarding War Diaries and Intelligence Summaries are contained in F. S. Regs., Part II. and the Staff Manual respectively. Title pages will be prepared in manuscript.

DADOS. 31 Division

WAR DIARY
or
~~INTELLIGENCE SUMMARY.~~

(Erase heading not required.)

July 1917.

Army Form C. 2118.

Place	Date	Hour	Summary of Events and Information	Remarks and references to Appendices
MARŒUIL	17.		Demand submitted for 300 Spare Boxes, Small Box Respirators. To replace & complete Reserve Extract Logwood 112 lbs & Bichromate of Potash 4 lbs demanded for staining tents in Divisional Area.	
	18		MOVE 243 Machine Gun Coy from Home.	
	19.		Demand received from B/170 Bde R.F.A. for 18 pdr. to replace E.O.C./3013 condemned for scoring. Demand submitted for four Clinometers for 243 Machine Gun Coy. First Supply under Q M G 17 (Q.A.3) 1/7/17.	
	20		Lieut E. G. Davies AOD granted 10 days leave	
	21		DM.2/230161 Driver Lynch J.R., 31 Divisional Supply Column, accidentally ~~[illegible]~~ wounded.	
	24.		MOVE. 318 Road Construction Coy R.E. from 1st Canadian Corps. Extract Logwood demanded on the 17th hastened.	
	25		8 Anti Aircraft Sights for Vickers Guns and 12 for Lewis Guns demanded under D.O.S. (O.S.B.1) 51/SP/29 25/7/17. 500 yards White Tape demanded to complete Establishment OS 14/226/1 21/7/17.	

A5834 Wt. W4973/M687 750,000 8/16 D. D. & L. Ltd. Forms/C.2118/13.

DADOS.
31 Division

Instructions regarding War Diaries and Intelligence Summaries are contained in F. S. Regs., Part II. and the Staff Manual respectively. Title pages will be prepared in manuscript.

WAR DIARY

~~or~~

~~INTELLIGENCE SUMMARY.~~

(Erase heading not required.)

July 1917.

Army Form C. 2118.

Place	Date	Hour	Summary of Events and Information	Remarks and references to Appendices
MARŒUIL	25		Large Demands for Paint received	
			Extract of Logwood Received & issued. Stencils for new Divisional Sign issued	
	27		Lieut E. G. DAVIES AOD returned from leave.	
	31		Demand received from B/165 Bde R.F.A for one Rangefinder Artillery No 1 to replace condemned.	

[signature]
Capt
DADOS 31 Divn.

A5834 Wt. W4973/M687 750,000 8/16 D. D. & L. Ltd. Forms/C.2118/13.

Confidential

Volume XX

Vol 18

War Diary.

D. A. D. O. S.

31st Division

August 1917.

Instructions regarding War Diaries and Intelligence Summaries are contained in F. S. Regs., Part II. and the Staff Manual respectively. Title pages will be prepared in manuscript.

WAR DIARY
or
INTELLIGENCE SUMMARY.
(Erase heading not required.)

D.A.D.O.S.
31 Divn
August 1917

Army Form C. 2118.

Place	Date	Hour	Summary of Events and Information	Remarks and references to Appendices
MAROEUIL	1		Move I/31 T.M.B. to 57. Division	
	3		1 Cart Officers Mess demanded for 127 Labour Coy. 1 Trench Mortar demanded for [93 T.M.B.	
	5		500 Waterproof Ration Bags demanded under A.R.O. 519-547.	
	8		Move 47 Labour Coy. to 2nd Division. 2 Machine Guns demanded for 92 M.G. Coy. to [replace L3835 + L3659 condemned.	
	10		Move 120 Labour Coy to O.O. 1st Corps Troops.	
	11		18 Fire Extinguishers demanded for D.A.C. (A.R.P.)	
	13		Received 62 No. 30 Periscopes from XIII Corps + issued 31 to 92 Inf/Bde + 31 to 94 Inf/Bde	
	14		6 Body Shields demanded for D.H.Q approved under G.R.O. 1133 by First Army O.S 48/24/11 [dated 11-8-17	
	15		1 Wagon Limbered G.S. hand demanded for 11 E. Lancs.	
	17		Demanded 500 Rattles for Gas Shell Alarm A.R.O. 1500 Authy. QMG 26/2/(Q.A.3) [dated 6-8-17	
	18		1 Cooks Cart demanded for 210 Field Coy R.E.	
	22		Received 500 Rattles for Gas Shell Alarm + issued them to Divl Gas Officer	
	23		D.D.O.S. First Army inspected Office, Armourers Shop, Old Clothing Store + Dump. 6 Extincteurs Fire demanded, approved under G.R.O. 1133 by First Army OS 48/701 [dated 21-8-17.	

A5834 Wt. W4973/M687 750,000 8/16 D. D. & L. Ltd. Forms/C.2118/13.

Instructions regarding War Diaries and Intelligence Summaries are contained in F. S. Regs., Part II. and the Staff Manual respectively. Title pages will be prepared in manuscript.

WAR DIARY
or
INTELLIGENCE SUMMARY.
(Erase heading not required.)

Contd. 2nd Sheet Army Form C. 2118.

August, 1917

Place	Date	Hour	Summary of Events and Information	Remarks and references to Appendices
23			One Machine Gun demanded for 92 M.G. Coy to replace one condemned by Divnl Armourer	
25			Machine Gun for 92 M.G. Coy received.	
26.			1 Cooks Cart demanded for 211 Field Coy R.E. 430 Greatcoats demanded for 42 Chinese Labour Coy. 1 Trench Mortar demanded for 93 T.M. Batty. to replace 2070 condemned [by I.O.M.	
27.			1500 Containers for S. Box Respirators demanded to replace Reserve of Old Pattern (Adv. G.H.Q. 10/17 (Q.A.3) d/16-7-17 + 17-8-17, First Army OS 48/90/58 [d/23-8-17.	
29.			Two Tents Marquee Small single demanded for storage accommodation under Q.M.G. 15/4 Q.A.3 d/25-8-17.	
			Move S/05720 Pte F.L. Mills + S/06660 Pte A.E. Johnson to Ordnance Havre (authy XIII Corps Telegram O.N. 881)	

N. A. Johnson Capt
D.A.D.O.S. 31 Divn.

A5834 Wt. W4973/M687 750,000 8/16 D. D. & L. Ltd. Forms/C.2118/13.

Confidential

Volume XXI

Vol 19

War Diary.

D. A. D. O. S. 31st Division

September 1917

Instructions regarding War Diaries and Intelligence Summaries are contained in F. S. Regs., Part II. and the Staff Manual respectively. Title pages will be prepared in manuscript.

Army Form C. 2118.

WAR DIARY or INTELLIGENCE SUMMARY.

(Erase heading not required.)

September 1917. DADOS 31st Divn

Place	Date	Hour	Summary of Events and Information	Remarks and references to Appendices
MAROEUIL	2nd		Wire to Base for one 3 inch Stokes T.M for 93 T.M Bty to replace one condemned.	
			30 Packs and 30 2 Gall Petrol Tins drawn from Salvage Officer for the purpose of making improvised hot food containers.	
	3rd		One 3 inch Stokes Trench Mortar received for 93 T.M Bty. Indent 31/4322 of 26/8/17.	
	4th		Wire to Base for one 3 inch Stokes T.M for 94 T.M Bty to replace condemned.	
	6th		S.D. Clothing issued to Batteries and Divnl Baths for the purpose of dealing with possible gas attacks.	
			48 Hat Irons received from Base	
	7th		56 and 36 Anti Aircraft sights for use with Vickers & Lewis Guns (respectively) demanded from Base.	
	10th		Wire to Base for 17540 N.C. Containers for Small Box Respirators.	
			One 3 inch Stokes T.M. received for 93 T.M. Bty.	
	11th		Alterations to 12 Tripods Auxiliary completed by the Divnl Armourers	

A5834 Wt. W4973/M687 750,000 8/16 D. D. & L. Ltd. Forms/C.2118/13.

Instructions regarding War Diaries and Intelligence Summaries are contained in F. S. Regs., Part II. and the Staff Manual respectively. Title pages will be prepared in manuscript.

WAR DIARY
or
INTELLIGENCE SUMMARY.
(Erase heading not required.)

Army Form C. 2118.

Place	Date	Hour	Summary of Events and Information	Remarks and references to Appendices
MARŒUIL	12th		One German Machine Gun surplus to establishment despatched to Base.	
			Capt. H.H. Johnson proceeds on leave	
	13th		Arrival. Lt E. G. Davies from Ord. 63 (RN) Div. to act for D.A.D.O.S. during Capt. H.H. Johnson's absence.	
			Wire to Base for 12300 Blankets to complete Div. to scale of one per man.	
	14th		30 Improvised Hot food containers ready for issue.	
			Wire to Base for one Carr QF 18 pr to replace one condemned for shell fire for B/165 Bde RFA	
	18th		60 No 22 and 60 No 24 Grenades Empty received from Base.	
	19th		Wire to Base for 19 Stewart Horse clipping machines & 57 spare heads.	
	21st		Demand sent to Base for 387½ Regs Horse.	
	23rd		Capt. H.H. Johnson returns from leave.	

A5834 Wt. W4973/M687 750,000 8/16 D. D. & L. Ltd. Forms/C.2118/13.

Instructions regarding War Diaries and Intelligence Summaries are contained in F. S. Regs., Part II. and the Staff Manual respectively. Title pages will be prepared in manuscript.

WAR DIARY
or
INTELLIGENCE SUMMARY.
(Erase heading not required.)

Army Form C. 2118.

Place	Date	Hour	Summary of Events and Information	Remarks and references to Appendices
MARIEUIL	23rd		Issue of 1st Blanket completed.	
			One 3 inch Stokes T.M. received for 94 T.M. Bty.	
	24th		2000 Boots Gum & 4000 Soles Inner demanded from Base.	
			19 Electric Horse Clipping Machines and Spare heads recd from Base	
			700 Ayrton Fans demanded from Base.	
			11 Lewis Guns received (thro' 31 Divl. H.Q.) for use against enemy aircraft	
	25th		16 Clinometers demanded from Base for Divl. Machine Gun Coys.	
	26th		Exchange of N.C. Containers for O.P. Containers for Box Respirators completed.	
	27th		Wire to Base for Winter Clothing (17000 bands body, 3400 Drawers Woollen and 17000 vests)	
	28th		700 Ayrton Fans received from Base.	
	30th		Wire to Base for 80 Vermorel Sprayers.	

7/10

H. Johnson Capt.
DADOS 31 Div

Confidential

Volume XXII

Vol 20

War Diary.

D. A. D. O. S. 31st Division

October 1917.

Sheet I

Instructions regarding War Diaries and Intelligence Summaries are contained in F. S. Regs., Part II. and the Staff Manual respectively. Title pages will be prepared in manuscript.

WAR DIARY
or
INTELLIGENCE SUMMARY.
(*Erase heading not required.*)

October 1917.
D.A.D.O.S. 31 Divn

Army Form C. 2118.

Place	Date	Hour	Summary of Events and Information	Remarks and references to Appendices
	2nd		Left for temporary duty at Havre Base.	
	3rd.		Visited all Groups at Base after reporting to C.O.O.	
			1602 prs Gum Boots received. One 9.45 Heavy T.M. No 964 received.	
	4th.		Visited Frouille & A.O.D. Workshops.	
			8000 Paillasses received from XIII Corps & Issued to Area Commandants.	
	5th.		Arrived back from Havre.	
			Wire for One 18 pr B/165 Bde replace 5464 (shell fire).	
	6th.		Demand 4500 prs Socks to complete Divnl Reserve.	
	7th.		Planned new site at ECURIE for Divnl. Ordnance.	
			Wire for One 4.5 how. replace 2066 (shell fire) for D/170 Bde.	
	8th.		Indent 12 Boxes Despatch for Infantry Battalions	
	9th.		Indent 38 Stoves Soyers to complete Divn to scale.	
			Indent 12 Rifles with Telescopic Sights for Infantry Battalions.	
			Indent 12 Pleyan Stereoscopes for Infantry Battalions	
			Indent 17000 Blankets (2nd Blanket) Authority First Army O.S. 7864 d/8-10-17.	
	10th.		Demand 400 Braziers, also Tools & Material for repair of Gum Boots.	
			MOVE Lieut E.G. DAVIES, A.O.D. to XIII Corps.	
	11th.		Demand 2000 prs Gum Boots & 4000 Soles Inner.	
			Wire for One 4.5 how. for D/170 Bde replace 1172 (shell fire).	

A5834 Wt. W4973/M687 750,000 8/16 D. D. & L. Ltd. Forms/C.2118/13.

Instructions regarding War Diaries and Intelligence Summaries are contained in F. S. Regs., Part II. and the Staff Manual respectively. Title pages will be prepared in manuscript.

Sheet II

WAR DIARY
or
INTELLIGENCE SUMMARY.

(Erase heading not required.)

October 1917
D.A.D.O.S. 31 Divn.

Army Form C. 2118.

Place	Date	Hour	Summary of Events and Information	Remarks and references to Appendices
	12th		Demand Two 3" T.M. replace 2728 and 2909 condemned for 92 T.M. Battery	
	13th		12 Boxes Disinfected received.	
	do.		38 Stoves Soyer received	
	14th		12 Rifles with Telescopic Sights + 12 Periscopes Stereoscopes received.	
	15th		400 Braziers received	
	16th		Demand One 3" T.M replace 1698 for 92 T.M. Battery.	
	17th		Received 17000 Blankets	
	do		Demand 12 Modified Jacks for removing Lewis Gun barrels	
	18th		Received 16 Chronometers for 4 Machine Gun Coys.	
	do.		Demand 2000 prs Gum Boots + 4000 Socks Inner	
	19th		Bulk Demand for Spectacles Tinted, Pliers Side cutting 8" + Shutters Signalling	
	do		Demand 100 Hot Food Containers Trade Pattern (Clock Hot Food Containers being made in Armourers Shop)	
	do.		Demand 4 Lewis Guns replace 3496, 1675, 3832 + 3699 (all condemned worn) for 92 M.G. Coy	
	20th		Received 4 Lewis Guns 4477, 4428, 4490 + 5584 for 92 M.G. Coy.	
	23rd		Demand Three 3" T.M for 93 T.M. Battery replace 1720, 4138, + 8 condemned.	
			Received Spectacles Tinted for 12 Infantry Battalions.	
			Received 12 Modified Jacks for removing L. G. barrels.	
			Received 2 3" T.M. 2295 + 3526 for 92 T.M. Battery	

A5834 Wt. W4973/M687 750,000 8/16 D. D. & L. Ltd. Forms/C.2118/13.

Instructions regarding War Diaries and Intelligence Summaries are contained in F. S. Regs., Part II. and the Staff Manual respectively. Title pages will be prepared in manuscript.

Sheet III

WAR DIARY
or
INTELLIGENCE SUMMARY.
(Erase heading not required.)

October 1917.
D.A.D.O.S. 31 Divn

Army Form C. 2118.

Place	Date	Hour	Summary of Events and Information	Remarks and references to Appendices
	24th		Demand One 3" for 92 T.M. Battery replace 2841 condemned.	
	do.		Received Two Sets Tools for repair of Gum Boots	
	25th		Demand for C/170 Bde One 18 pdr replace 6130 (shell fire).	
	do.		Demand for C/170 Bde One 18 pdr Carriage replace C.25491 (shell fire)	
	26th		Capt C.F. Hartung A.O.D. from Base Store visited the Division, + went to ECURIE Railhead	
	do.		Demand for C/170 Bde One 18 pdr and Carriage replace 6279 and 46000 (shell fire).	
	do.		Received One 3" T.M. 6411 for 92 T.M. Battery.	
	27th		Capt C.F. Hartung A.O.D visited Div. Clean Clothing Store, Salvage, Ordnance Dumps, Armrs. Shop, Old Clothing Store. Demand Leather Jerkins etc from Base.	
	28th		Demand 218 Bags Waterproof. Capt C.F. Hartung visited XIII Corps Laundry, + Amm.n Railhead.	
	do.		Capt C.F. Hartung left for 4th Division.	
	29th		Four 3" T.M. received (3 for 93 T.M. Battery, 1 for 92 T.M. Battery).	
	31st		Bulk Demand to Base for initial issue of Horse Shoes fitted with Frost Cogs.	

J.H. Johnson Capt.
D.A.D.O.S. 31 Divn

A5834 Wt. W4973/M687 750,000 8/16 D. D. & L. Ltd. Forms/C.2118/13.

Confidential

Volume XXIII

Vol ~~3~~ 21

War Diary.

D. A. D. O. S. 31st Division

November 1917.

Sheet I

Instructions regarding War Diaries and Intelligence Summaries are contained in F. S. Regs., Part II. and the Staff Manual respectively. Title pages will be prepared in manuscript.

November 1917

WAR DIARY
or
INTELLIGENCE SUMMARY.
(Erase heading not required.)

D.A.D.O.S. 31 Divn

Army Form C. 2118.

Place	Date	Hour	Summary of Events and Information	Remarks and references to Appendices
MAROEUIL	2		Indent to Base for 8 Pistols Signals 1½" for issue 1 per Bty. R.F.A.	
	3		Wire to Base for 2 3" Stokes T.M. replace 3893 + 417 condemned (92 T.M.B)	
	4		Demand submitted to Base for Tent Bottom Sets	
	5		Wire to Base for 1 3" Stokes T.M. replace 859 condemned (92 T.M.B)	
	6		Indent Mountings Trench 17 and Overbank 6	
	7		Indent to Base for Screws & Chains to Ster Dials Elevating MK IV tripod Vickers Guns	
			Received from Base 8 1½" Pistols Signal	
ECURIE	8		MOVE to site near ECURIE Railhead.	
			500 Hammocks received from XIII Corps Troops	
			Exchange of Shears wire cutting 5" for 8" completed	
	10		Demand received from 2/165 for one QF 18 pdr replace 5416 condemned Dvn	
	12		3 3" Stokes T.M.'s received for 92 T.M.B.	
	13		Wire to Base for 4 3" Stokes T.M. replace 6411, 374, 253 + 630 destroyed	
			Indent to Base for 150 Yukon Packs to complete Divn to scale.	
			Indent to Base for 600 tins for carriage of Water	
	14		Demand to Base for 24 Lanterns Bullseye for distribution to 4 M.G. Coys	
			Indent 5000 Cartridges S.A. Blank	

A5834 Wt. W4973/M687 750,000 8/16 D. D. & L. Ltd. Forms/C.2118/13.

Sheet II

Instructions regarding War Diaries and Intelligence Summaries are contained in F. S. Regs., Part II. and the Staff Manual respectively. Title pages will be prepared in manuscript.

November

WAR DIARY
or
INTELLIGENCE SUMMARY.
(Erase heading not required.)

D.A.D.O.S. 31 Divn.

Army Form C. 2118.

Place	Date	Hour	Summary of Events and Information	Remarks and references to Appendices
ECURIE	15		D.A.D.O.S. to No 14 Ord Depot for course of instruction in Ammunition.	
			Pte R.H. CHAPLIN No. 06356 A.O.C. wounded	
	17		Two keys received for opening Ammunition Boxes fitted with Butterfly Nuts.	
	18		Four 3" Stokes T.M.'s received from 92 T.M.B.	
			Indent to Base for 120 Dummy Grenades (empty) No 23 with dummy igniters	
	19		Wire for one 3" Stokes T.M. to replace No. 2295 condemned (93 T.M.B.)	
			24 [illegible] received for M.G. Coys	
	25		One 3" Stokes received for 93 T.M.B.	
	27		Indent to Base for 212 Bags Waterproof to replace similar number condemned.	
	28		Indent to Base for 36 Modified Jacks for removal of L.G. barrels to complete to [illegible]	
			Census of Guns & Carriages in possession of Divisional Artillery	
	29		Bulk Indent to Base for 141 Leather jerkins for issue to M.G. Coys & T.M.B.'s	
	30		Indent to Base for 400 Horse [illegible] Brushes	
			Indent Canvas [illegible] 300 yds for issue to Inf. Bdes.	

[signature] Capt
DADOS 31 Divn.

A5834 Wt. W4973/M687 750,000 8/16 D. D. & L. Ltd. Forms/C.2118/13.

Confidential

Volume XXIV

Vol 22

War Diary.

D. A. D. O. S. 31st Division

December 1917.

O/c Records AOC
thro' O/c A.O.C Section G.H.Q
3rd Echelon B.E.F.

D.A.G. 3rd Echelon

—

Herewith please find War Diary for A.O. Corps 31st Divn for month of December 1917.

J. Whelugee Captain
DAC
for Lieut Col. AA & QMG
31st Divn

for Capt.
DADOS 31 Div

Instructions regarding War Diaries and Intelligence Summaries are contained in F. S. Regs., Part II. and the Staff Manual respectively. Title pages will be prepared in manuscript.

WAR DIARY
or
INTELLIGENCE SUMMARY.
(Erase heading not required.)

Army Form C. 2118.

December 1917

DADOS 31 Division

Place	Date	Hour	Summary of Events and Information	Remarks and references to Appendices
Ecoivre	1/12/17		Captain N H JOHNSON AOD DADOS 31st Division rejoined from Ammunition Course – Awarded Pass 80% Marks. 12 K.O.Y.L.I. (Pioneer Bn) rejoined Divn from 50th Divn. MOVE order notified all concerned on 5/12/17. Batman to Capt. N.H. Johnson AOD rejoined staff of DADOS 31 Divn. Post on strength. Following units transferred from 21st Divn to 31st Divn – Move order sent all concerned. 25 MAC, No 5 DSC, 33 OMW, HQ 25 Labour Gp, 149 Labour Coy, 341 Road Constn Coy.	
	2/12/17		New pattern of Trench Boots received for trial. Indent for 1.18 pdr for C/165 to replace 5099 removed – Condemned Scoring – Wire Indent 31/7/12	
	4.12.		Instns. from DADOS XIII Corps re special precautions for preservation of M.T. Vehicles during frosty weather received and communicated to ASC MT attached who are fully cognisant of what is required of them & are qualified to take correct action. Indent from C170 for 1-18 pdr to replace 5744 – Condemned Scoring – Wire Indent 31/753. Move of 5th DSC to 47 Divn. All concerned notified.	
	5/12		One Wagon G.S. demanded 3 Section DAC. Wire Indent 31/834 5th. One Wagon pontoon R.E. 211 Fd Coy R.E. Wire Indent 31/783/5th.	
	6/12		One 3 inch Stokes Mortar demanded on Wire Indent 875/6th replace 845 condemned by SOME. 4 P.B. men sent to Employment Base Etaples Authy CR 32001/36C/30th.	
	7/12		One Wagon G.S. demanded for 2 Section DAC. Wire Indent 31/915/7th.	
Marœuil	8/12		3 Chaff cutters for A, B & C Batteries 165 Bde to complete units in Divn to scale QMG 57 (QA3) 1/11/17. Office & Dump moved from ECOIVRE to MAROEUIL.	
	10/12		06356 Pte CHAPLIN RH – Classified Battle Casualty – Invalided to England 11/17 vide OIC Records GHQ AOC 1753 3/12/17. AOC 31 Divn.	

Army Form C. 2118.

WAR DIARY
or
INTELLIGENCE SUMMARY.
(*Erase heading not required.*)

Instructions regarding War Diaries and Intelligence Summaries are contained in F. S. Regs., Part II. and the Staff Manual respectively. Title pages will be prepared in manuscript.

Place	Date	Hour	Summary of Events and Information	Remarks and references to Appendices
Mareuil	10/12/17		A1965 Armourer Sgt EDWARDS A.O.C (18th West Yorkshire Regt) attached DADOS 31 Div admitted to H.	
			Winter Clothing - Indent submitted for Leather Jerkins 31/988 (10/12/17). 3862 demanded for 12 KOYLI + Artillery Bde.	
			Anti-gas Stores - Indent submitted for 200 Blankets for Dugouts. 31/918/10/12/17.	
			One 4.5 inch Howitzer demanded for D.165 Bde RFA. 31/990/10/12/17 replace 6?1 condemned [illegible]	
	11/12/17		Armr Sgts instructed to inspect Rifles, M. Guns, + Lewis Guns of 94 Infy Bde on 12, 13, 14 & 15 Dec. 17.	
			17 West Yorks Regt joined 31st Division from 35 Div. Surplus Stores utilised off outstanding Indents + balance afterwards despatched to Base. Vehicles handed in to Comm under Special Instrns. Secret O.B. 1370/10 9/17 + 2nd Army O.S. 48/957/7/10/17 + 1510 (G) 11/9/17 XIII Corps (OB/753)/5 from ADOS and XIII Corps Q 1687 and 31 Div 31 D/S543/12 A. and D.D.S.T. 2nd Army 1416/17/8/10/17 Vehicles being utilised off Indents. 15 Lewis Guns + Equipment being overhauled at 31 Divl Armourers Shop preparatory to return to Ordnance Depot	
	13/12/17		One 6 inch Newton Mortar recd off Indent 31/681/30/11/17. Regn No. 1174.	
	14/12/17		Tripod Mk IV for Gr M.G.C demanded replace condemned - 31/1050/14/12/17	
			16000 Covers for Steel Helmets demanded under GRO 2944 - only 1744 issued by Base.	
			6 inch Newton Mortar beds complete 2 demanded for Z 31 TMB to replace unserviceable 31/1084/14/12/17	
ECURIE	15/12/17		Office and Dump moved from Mareuil to Ecurie. Divl Bootmakers - 5 men set to work on repair under supervision of DADOS 31 Div - previously under Camp Comdt 31 Div. Armourers Shop in course of erection under arrangements by CRE 31st Div. Meanwhile 31 Divl Armourers remain in Old Shop at Mareuil.	

A5834 Wt. W4973/M687 750,000 8/16 D. D. & L. Ltd. Forms/C.2118/13.

Army Form C. 2118.

Instructions regarding War Diaries and Intelligence Summaries are contained in F. S. Regs., Part II. and the Staff Manual respectively. Title pages will be prepared in manuscript.

WAR DIARY
or
INTELLIGENCE SUMMARY.
(Erase heading not required.)

Place	Date	Hour	Summary of Events and Information	Remarks and references to Appendices
ECURIE	16/12/17		One 3inch Stokes Mortar received off Indent 31/875/6/12/17 for 9? T.M.B (No 604 2 recd replace 345)	
	17/12/17		Scarcity of App. Sights Dial illuminating & Aiming Point Sets:- Batteries - full particulars given to ADOS XIII Corps resulting in Siege lamps being offered as a temporary measure - RFA Batteries agreed but desired that their Indents for Electric Batteries requisite should stand - to be supplied as and when available	
	18/12/17		No 235072 Pte. R. THOMPSON - 2nd Seaforth Highrs - reported for duty from 1st Army Troops authy - 1st Army C.S. 9374/16/12/17.	
			4.5 How. D165 available off Indent 31/990/10/12/17. [illegible] Ord. Gen Park No 1 instructed [illegible] to draw 4.5 How. of 31/990 - Drawn & reported all concerned - delivered to Ion. 1 BOMW(L) Regd No 2378 in replacement of 571	
			Change of Base from Havre & Rouen to Calais [illegible] Authy D.O.S. A 432/15/12/17. Bases concerned notified to transfer Indents accordingly. All concerned notified	
	19/12/17		No 27905 Pte. Pollard 10th Scottish Rifles - reported for duty under DADOS 31 Div. Authy OC C 3200/360/30/11/17. THAW PRECAUTIONS instns as to received. Store Tent pitched at Railhead in readiness for dumping stores likely to be required whilst Thaw precautions are in progress.	
	20/12/17		Thaw Precautions cancelled - As Ordnance Dump is close to Railhead & the route is well metalled - little inconvenience is anticipated whilst present Ordnance Dump is retained. Cart O.M. awarded for C 165 Bde RFA replace Condemned - 31/1250/20/12/17	
			Reports re [illegible] Cogs - Position of Division regarding possession of these - Good. No complaints to date	

A5834 Wt. W4973/M687 750,000 8/16 D. D. & L. Ltd. Forms/C.2118/13.

Instructions regarding War Diaries and Intelligence Summaries are contained in F. S. Regs., Part II. and the Staff Manual respectively. Title pages will be prepared in manuscript.

WAR DIARY
or
INTELLIGENCE SUMMARY.
(Erase heading not required.)

Army Form C. 2118.

Place	Date	Hour	Summary of Events and Information	Remarks and references to Appendices
ECOIVRE	20/12/17		31 D.A. H.Q. asked as to number of Air Recuperators in possession with a view to checking their Indents for Lever Compressors - Reply 8 in possession.	
	21/12/17		Indents for Visor Rifle Grenade - 1 per M.G.C. demanded 31/1946 also Demand for Surcingles [illegible] for [illegible] M.G.C. 31/1947.	
	22/12/17		Indent 31/1297 - One 18 pdr for B170 - D.D.O.S. Army instructed Cancel Indent 23/12/17 Gun to replace 4194 already demanded by Canadian Divn.	
			Indent 31/1793 - One Wagon Limbered Body R.E. demanded for 31 Divl Signal Coy.	
	23/12/17		Owing to continuance of Frost and instructions from A.D.O.S. XIII Corps to keep sufficient Frost Cogs ready to cope with demands of units when & if transport from Base of supplies [illegible] through weather conditions - a demand on Wire Indent 31/1310/23rd inst was sent Base for 15 cwts of 1/2 inch and 8 Cwts of 3/8" - In addition to those already on Bulk Indents due to Divn.	
	23/12/17		Cut Offs removal from Rifles other than those of Cavalry Regts. - Returns called for & arrangements made to deal with number for alteration at 31 Divl Armrs Shop	
	24/12/17		Indent 31/1837/24/12/17 to Base - One 4.5 inch Carriage replace 26273 condemned Shell [illegible] - D165 Bde	
	25/12/17		Indent 31/1347/25/12 to Gun Park No 1 for D165 Bde R.F.A. for 1 Sight dial No 7 + Carrier for ditto replace condemned.	
	26/12/17		12 K.O.Y.L.I. report that Frost Cogs are made of very soft material and a sample was sent of some worn out after a journey of only 8 1/2 miles. Units Complaint & Frost Cogs despatched A.D.O.S. for information.	
	27/12/17		Wired Calais pointing out urgency re supply of Frost Cogs to keep units going. Wire O259/27/12/17.	
			Captain N.H. Johnson D.A.D.O.S. 31 Divn. authorised to proceed on leave to U.K.	
			Indent submitted Base for 200 Blankets G.S. for Dug Outs - (Anti gas protection) Reason for demand - Cloth Union A.G. authorised by G.R.O. 2994 not available from R.E. sources within the Army	

A5834 Wt. W4973/M687 750,000 8/16 D. D. & L. Ltd. Forms/C.2113/13.

Instructions regarding War Diaries and Intelligence Summaries are contained in F. S. Regs., Part II. and the Staff Manual respectively. Title pages will be prepared in manuscript.

WAR DIARY
or
INTELLIGENCE SUMMARY.
(Erase heading not required.)

Army Form C. 2118.

Place	Date	Hour	Summary of Events and Information	Remarks and references to Appendices
ECURIE	27 12/17		Indent 31/1365 sent Base for Overalls white, Covers white drill for Steel Helmets Covers Rifle Snow Vide G.R.O. 3010	
			Indent 31/1454 sent Base for 752 prs F.S. Boots size 7 - due to Divn & not supplied by last Base - not Shewn on dues out list from Old Base. Rouen agree on their C.I. 348 (G.R.O. 2621.)	
	28 12/17		Calais asked to send all stores available - Frost Cogs urgently required (O/260/28 12/17.)	
	28 12/17		Capt N.H. Johnson AOD DADOS 31 Div proceeded to Base Port for leave to U.K. (14 days from 29th 12/17)	
			Colonel W.H. Annesley AA & QMG. 31 Divn. taking over his duties in the interim	
			Indent Wire 31/1409/28 12/17 to all concerned for 2 - 18 por Barrels replace 430 + 3362 also 2 18 por Carriages replace 43676 and 39386 - condemned Shell Fire.	
			Calais asked which particular Indents - nos given on Wire O269/28 12/17 - to supply Frost Cogs + Blankets for Dug Outs.	
	29 12/17		Indent wire 31/1431/29 12/17 on Gun Park for Mounting Tripod IV. replace destroyed Shell fire } - 94 M.G.C.	
			Indent wire 31/1433/29 12/17 on Base for 3 inch Stokes Barrel mk replace 2147 condemned - for 93 L.T.M.B.	
			Indent wire 31/1434/29 12/17 on Gun Park No 1 for 4 Rods Cleaning - One Base Cap - one Pin's Striker replace unserviceable } - " -	
			Indent wire 31/1437/29 12/17 " " " " for Sight dial No 7 and Carrier for ditto (18 por) replace 5614 and 107 Condemned on Gorm's Certificate for Shell Fire for C165 Bde R.F.A.	
			Indent wire 31/1438 for C165 Bde R.F.A. to Base for Case No 7 dial Sight and Carrier Q.F. 13 + 18 pdr I - Shell fire	
	30 12/17		Calais informed on Wire O271/30 12/17 that Divn can accept as much as can be sent off Indents. (Q.C. 4509/29.12.17. Issue being made on 30th of Horseshoes etc - Frost Cogs demanded not available.)	
			Calais message re Frost Cogs demanded not being available notified to A.D.O.S. XIII Corps + DHQ - A.D.O.S. XIII Corps instructions on Wire O.N. 290/30 12/17 to demand Frost Nails in lieu - Wire Indent 31/1476/30 12/17 for estimated requirements to units sent Base - No previous Indents cancelled pending question of supply being placed on a good basis.	
			Base wire 3 Trucks on Rail with Horseshoes &c for Divn & later that 89 bls Frost Cogs had been loaded - these being all that were available.	
	31 12/17		15 LEWIS Guns handed over to Ord. Gun Park No 1.	
			Indent 31/1505 Wired Base for 300 yards Canvas for 3 Fd. Ambulances.	

A5834 Wt. W4973/M687 750,000 8/16 D. D. & L. Ltd. Forms/C. 2118/13.

Sheet I

Instructions regarding War Diaries and Intelligence Summaries are contained in F. S. Regs., Part II. and the Staff Manual respectively. Title pages will be prepared in manuscript.

WAR DIARY
or
INTELLIGENCE SUMMARY.
(Erase heading not required.)

January 1918.

Army Form C. 2118.

D.A.D.O.S. 31 Div.

Vol 23

Place	Date	Hour	Summary of Events and Information	Remarks and references to Appendices
ECURIE	1-1-18		Two Sections join 92 and 93 M.G. Coy to complete them to W.E.	
			Wire 0281 to O.O. No. 8 Regulating Station to trace trucks 129719, 61358, 414 containing urgent stores	
	3-1-18		Indent 31/1310 for Frost Cogs Lactred.	
			Indent 31/1578 for one 18 pdr. for B/170 to replace 3659 condemned Scoring.	
			Indent 31/1579 for one 18 pdr. for C/170 to replace 4984 Scoring.	
			Wire to 31 Div. Arty (0285) that 6 - 18pdr carriages and 1 - 4.5 carriage due to complete [including those in Shops	
	4-1-18		Indent 31/1480 for one Wagon G.S. Mk X for No 2 Coy Div Train.	
	5-1-18		Indent 31/1624 for Composees Liquid to complete under G.R.O. 3025.	
			" 31/1626 for Gloves Moleskin to complete under G.R.O. 2950	
			" 31/1627 for Brushes Dandy Small to complete under 1st Army R.O. 2120.	
	6-1-18		" 31/1648 for 5000 rds. Blank S.A.A. to replace used in training.	
			" 31/1611 for Wagon Limbered R.E. Body for 211 Field Coy R.E. replace condemned	
			" 31/1650 for One Cart Water Tank for 12 K.O.Y.L.I. replace condemned	
			Received One 18 pdr for B/170 off indent 2CN/5435 d/19-12-17	
	8-1-18		~~Received~~ " " " " " 31/1578 d/3-1-18 (No. 5006)	
			" " " " C/170 " 31/1579 d/3-1-18 ~~(No. 5006)~~ N.A. (No. 4268)	
			Wire 0298 for 200 Blankets for protection of Dug-outs G.R.O. 2904	
			Indent 31/1696 - 92 T.M.B. for one Stokes Mortar Barrel to replace 3600 condemned	
			Received 2 - 18 pdrs and carriages Nos. 2621, + 8140 and C 33386 and 4783 off indent [31/1409.	

A5834 Wt. W4973/M687 750,000 8/16 D. D. & L. Ltd. Forms/C.2118/13.

Sheet 2.

WAR DIARY
or
INTELLIGENCE SUMMARY.
(Erase heading not required.)

Army Form C. 2118.

January 1918

D.A.D.O.S. 31 Divn.

Instructions regarding War Diaries and Intelligence Summaries are contained in F. S. Regs., Part II. and the Staff Manual respectively. Title pages will be prepared in manuscript.

Place	Date	Hour	Summary of Events and Information	Remarks and references to Appendices
ECURIE	12-1-18		Indent 31/1768 for 4473 Leather Jerkins or Undercoats Fur - G.R.O. 3023	
	13-1-18		" 31/1769 for 9018 Gloves/Fingerless - G.R.O. 3072	
			CAPT. N. H. JOHNSON returned from Leave	
	14-1-18		Indent 31/1813 for 5000 rounds Blank S.A.A. for Training.	
			Meeting of Quartermasters & Q.M. Sergeants to discuss Returns of Unserviceable Items.	
			G.R.O. 2134 - Units called upon for Returns of Horse Respirators in possession.	
			Indent 31/1816 for one Stokes Mortar Barrel for 92 T.M.B. to replace 719 condemned	
			Indent 31/1819 for one 18 pdr. for A/170 to replace 5281 provisionally condemned	
			Indent 31/1818 for two 18 pdrs. for C/170 to replace 393 & 5064. provisionally condemned (O.M. G. 208 (P.B.3) 15.2.17)	
			" 31/1817 for one 18 pdr for B/165 to replace 386 provisionally condemned - Setting	
	15-1-18		Indent 31/1849 for 3600 Blankets to bring Units up to Establishment.	
			Received Stokes Mortar Barrel for 92 T.M.B., for Indent 31/1696.	
	16-1-18		THAW PRECAUTIONS.	
	19-1-18		Four 18 pdrs received off Indents 31/1817, 8, and 9.	
			Indent 31/1955 for hind portion of Wagon Limbered G.S. to replace 13207 condemned.	
	20-1-18		Indent O 330 for Body Kitchen Travg. for 11 E. Lancs to replace it.	
	21-1-18		Indent 31/2014 for Two Stokes Mortar Barrels for 92 T.M.B. to replace 187 & 3944 condemned.	
	22-1-18		One Stokes Mortar Barrel received off Indent 31/1433	
			Ptes R Thompson 2 Seaforth Highlanders (235072) and Pollard 10 Scottish Rifles (27905) returned to their Base Depot Authy First Army Q3 10/791 d/1-1-18.	

A5834 Wt. W4973/M687 750,000 8.16 D. D. & L. Ltd. Forms/C.2118/13.

Stat 3.

Instructions regarding War Diaries and Intelligence Summaries are contained in F. S. Regs., Part II. and the Staff Manual respectively. Title pages will be prepared in manuscript.

WAR DIARY
or
INTELLIGENCE SUMMARY.
(Erase heading not required.)

Army Form C. 2118.

January 1918
D.A.D.O.S. 31 Div.

Place	Date	Hour	Summary of Events and Information	Remarks and references to Appendices
ECURIE	28		Thaw Precautions off.	
			Indent 31/2129 Stokes Mortar Barrel One for 94 T.M.B. to replace 2543 condemned.	
			" 31/2130 for One Wagon G.S. MK X for No 3 Sec D.A.C.	
	28		ARMOURERS SHOP moved from MAROEUIL to ECURIE	
	29		Bulk Indents sent D.R.L.S. instead of by WIRE, as had been done during inclement weather.	
	30		Received Two Stokes Mortar Barrels against Ind. 31/2014	
			Store Tents pitched to accommodate returned Stores of Battalions disbanded.	

J. A. Johnson Capt
D.A.D.O.S. 31 Div.

Instructions regarding War Diaries and Intelligence Summaries are contained in F. S. Regs., Part II. and the Staff Manual respectively. Title pages will be prepared in manuscript.

February 1918.

WAR DIARY
or
INTELLIGENCE SUMMARY.
(*Erase heading not required.*)

D.A.D.O.S.
31st Division

Army Form C. 2118.

Vol 24

Place	Date	Hour	Summary of Events and Information	Remarks and references to Appendices
ECURIE.	1st		Wire to base for two 3" Stokes T.M. for 92 T.M. Btty to replace Nos 5397 & 299 Condemned	
			Indent to Base for one Wagon R.E. Body for 210th Coy R.E. & one Kitchen Travelling Body for 11th E. Lancs Regt	
	3rd		Indent to Base for Butt Catches & Milled Thumb pieces to enable alteration to be [illegible]	
	4th		Indent 150 pairs gum boots to replace unserviceable	
	6th		Two 3" Stokes T.M's received for 92 TM Btty	
	7th		Wire one 3" Stokes TM for 92 Inf Batty to replace No 1398 Condemned.	
	8th		MOVE. 3rd Coldstream Guards to 31st Div from Guards Div	
			Wire to D.A.G. Base for 3 reinforcements to complete establishment	
	9th		All indents for 18 West Yorks, & 12th & 13th E Yorks Cancelled on Base.	
	10th		Indent 120 prs gum boots to replace unserviceable.	
			Surplus stores of 18th W. Yorks returned to Base	
	12th		One 3" Stokes No 1277 received for 92 TM Btty.	
			Wire One Camp Officers' Mess No 5/70 to replace condemned.	
			MOVE 4th Grenadier Guards & 2nd Irish Gds to 31st Div from Guards Brigade	
	14th		Wire for one Wagon G.S. for No 3 Coy 31 D.A.C. to replace condemned.	
			All Indents cancelled on Base for 12 & 14 Yorks: Lancs & 16 W Yorks Regt.	

Instructions regarding War Diaries and Intelligence Summaries are contained in F. S. Regs., Part II. and the Staff Manual respectively. Title pages will be prepared in manuscript.

WAR DIARY
or
INTELLIGENCE SUMMARY.
(Erase heading not required.)

Army Form C. 2118.

Place	Date	Hour	Summary of Events and Information	Remarks and references to Appendices
ECURIE	15.2.		Arrival of Lieut W.H. Swallow A.O.D. from Calais, for Instruction in the Duties of Div. Ord. Officer	
			Surplus Stores from 16 W York Regt returned to Base.	
	16.2.			
	19.2.		Wire Two 3" Stokes T.M. for 92 T M Batty to replace Nos. 2152 + 3878 Condemned	
	20.2.		92 M.G. Coy report two Vickers Guns out of action; These were repaired in Div. Armourers' Shop.	
			Formation of V/XIII Heavy T.M. Batty being Completed from V/31, V/56, + V/62 H.T.M. Batteries.	
	21.2.		Wire to Gun Park for 50 wire cutters, reqd by 92 Brigade for Special purpose.	
			96 Lewis Guns received from disbanded Battalions, cleaned, overhauled + tested in Div Armr's Shop for issue of Scale 'A' Anti-aircraft: 30 for 31st Div. 30 for 56 Div. 23 for XIII Corps Troops, + 13 returned to Ord. Gun Pk No 1	
	22.2.		Wire for one 3" Stokes T. Mortar to replace No. 4053 Condemned.	
			230 Tents C.S.L. returned to Base by 6 Labour Coys administered by this Div.	
	23.2.		3 Reinforcements A.O.C. arrive from Base.	
			Indent 2500 Covers for Steel Helmets to complete Div.	
	24.2.		Two 3" Stokes T. Mortars received for 92 T.M. Battery.	
			Wire One 3" Stokes T.M. for 92 T.M. Battery to replace No. 1277 Condemned.	
			Indent 23 Yukon Packs to complete Division to scale	
	25.2.		Captain N.H. JOHNSON A.O.D. granted Special leave for 10 days. LIEUT W.H. SWALLOW left in charge.	
	26.2.		Statement to XIII Corps showing requirements of Div. to complete to Scale 'B' Anti-aircraft	
			Wire one 3" Stokes T. Mortar for 94 T.M. Batty to replace No 5671 Condemned.	
	27.2.		One 3" Stokes T. Mortar No 2956 received for 92 T.M. Batty.	
	28.2.		Wire one 3" Stokes T. Mortar for 92 T.M. Batty. to replace 4795 Condemned	
			Issue of 30 Lewis Guns for A.A. completed.	
			4.3.18	

W.H. Swallow Lieut
for D.A.D.O.S.
31st Division

A5834 Wt. W4973/M687 750,000 8/16 D. D. & L. Ltd. Forms/C.2118/13.

Instructions regarding War Diaries and Intelligence Summaries are contained in F. S. Regs., Part II. and the Staff Manual respectively. Title pages will be prepared in manuscript.

WAR DIARY
or
~~INTELLIGENCE SUMMARY.~~

(Erase heading not required.)

Army Form C. 2118.

DADOS 31 D
Vol 25

Place	Date	Hour	Summary of Events and Information	Remarks and references to Appendices
Ecurie	1st March 18		26 Sprats drawn from Gun Pk 1. to complete units to Scale "B". Issued between 2nd & 11th. Question of sights Dial No 7 taken up with HQ Divl. Arty.	QMG 53/10 QB3 6.2.18
	2nd		Notified 31 Div HQ. of receipt of important stores returned by two of the disbanded Battns. Calais asked re the formation of new Battn M.G Corps from the present 4 M.G Coys. Asked DHQ for all information available.	
Tinques	3rd		Moved to Tinques - taking over from 62nd Div. Accommodation provided most unsuitable. Pointed this out to 'Q' who agreed. Balance of stores, on account of reduction of 12 KOYLI to a 3 Co. basis dispatched to base. Indent for one 18 pdr to replace 5252 for C/170 Bde R.F.A.	GHQ 4788 (QA1)
	4th		Indent for above gun cancelled. Received Stokes barrels off indent 6442 for 94 T.M.B.	
	5th		Following units moved to 62 Div: 21 Lab. Group, HQs Nos 2, 127, 147, 169, 179 L. Coys. 42 Chinese Lab. Coy. 318 + 341 Road Construction Coy. 176 Tunnelling Co. 33. Ord Mob. Workshop + 25 M.A.C.	
	6th		Notified by Corps that guns of Divs. would be handed over in "situ". 25 Lab Group HQ moved to 1st Army Corps.	
	8th		92 93 94 + 243 MGC disbanded to form 31 Battn MG Corps. Base notified to cancel indents for [illegible] only, & to amend other indents to read 31st Batt. M.G. Corps. Travelling Kitchen of KOYLI sent to base.	
	9th		A.S.S. Evans appointed for permanent duty as Armourer	DAG GHQ 9/8017/d. 20/3/18
			Clock put forward at 11 pm one hour. Summer time	
	10th		Corps informed me Mob. store table for new M G Battn not yet available. Matter taken up with Army. 5 Lewis Guns from 12 KOYLI returned to Div Armr for overhaul. Issued on 12th. Two other Lewis guns of 12 KOYLI returned & question referred to Corps whether they should be reissued as A. A. guns.	
	11		First Army OS 48/1016 of 8 inst & XIII Corps OK 892/S received stating that these two guns must be returned to Base.	

A5834 Wt. W4973/M687 750,000 8/16 D. D. & L. Ltd. Forms/C.2118/13.

Instructions regarding War Diaries and Intelligence Summaries are contained in F. S. Regs., Part II. and the Staff Manual respectively. Title pages will be prepared in manuscript.

WAR DIARY
or
~~INTELLIGENCE SUMMARY.~~

(Erase heading not required.)

Army Form C. 2118.

Place	Date	Hour	Summary of Events and Information	Remarks and references to Appendices
Duisans [illegible]	Mar	12	Report on Zentage cutter for trenches to ADOS XIII Corps. Corps informed position re Sights Dial No. 7 – three reqd to complete & issued to C/165, D/165 & C/170. Informed Corps that no cases had cropped up where rifle stocks had split or stock bolts had broken when firing present pattern of Rifle Grenade. Carts Cook surplus through formation of 31st M.G. Corps sent to base.	
		13	Two screw jacks 20 Ton returned to Gun Park from V/XIII T.M.B. Question taken up with Div Arty as to return of certain stores by 62 D.A. which stores have been handed over to outgoing batteries. This caused me a good deal of unnecessary work.	
		14	Captain N. H. Johnson granted an extension of leave to 23rd inst. (DDOS 1st Army, OS 46/143. d. 13/3/18). Question of deficiencies – principal items of disbanded Battns going into & report submitted to 31 D.H.Q. under DOS. OSA 1/573 (A3) 3.3.18	
		16	Instructions given re the 7 Hotchkiss guns authorised under 1st Army OS 8/192/3 of 12th inst. Res of these have been drawn & issued. One gun only to M.T. Column (now Coy) as laid down in XIII C.O.A 23/11/3 d 16/3	
		17.	Wired Balan of dispatch of 2 Lewis guns, surplus from 12 KOYLI (See note 11th inst) & two Lewis M. Guns 4/7 Heavy Ft.	
		18	Letter from XIII Corps advising re-organisation of M.T. units. Base to be informed & all outstanding indents to be cancelled, & fresh ones submitted for actual requirements.	
		20	Indent for 24 Jump lines to complete to scale Q.M.G. 33/10. Q.A. 3. 15.2.18	
		21	31 Div A wire AA 307. to pack up & be ready to move on further instructions. Wire 0544 to O. Balan, O. Gun Park 1. to stop issues from to day. Wire 0548 to all Concerned to transfer indents from XIII Corps 1st Army to VI Corps 3 Army	

A5834 Wt. W4973/M687 750,000 8/16 D. D. & L. Ltd. Forms/C.2118/13.

Army Form C. 2118.

Instructions regarding War Diaries and Intelligence Summaries are contained in F. S. Regs., Part II. and the Staff Manual respectively. Title pages will be prepared in manuscript.

WAR DIARY
or
INTELLIGENCE SUMMARY.
(Erase heading not required.)

Place	Date	Hour	Summary of Events and Information	Remarks and references to Appendices
	23 March		Came under administration of 6 Corps 3rd Army. Ordered to be prepared to move at short notice. Calais wired O.C. 6587 cancelling all bulk stores & asking if prepared to receive gun stores. Replied Yes. Wired to O.O. Gun Park No 1. to supply as many gun stores as possible off indents to 22nd inst.	
Douchy les Ayette	24 March		Moved to this place. Two lorries promised by DHQ to assist did not materialise. Visited by A.D.O.S VI Corps. Wire O.55 q to Calais to say can receive gun stores.	
Humbercamps	25 March		Under two hours notice to move. Move commenced at 11 pm to Humbercamps. A.D.O.S called with list of 3 Army Gun Park stores. Copied this & passed it to D.A.D.O.S 42nd Div. Wired Havre to issue only important stores, vehicles &c until further orders. Authority from 6 Corps to draw 50 tents C.S.L. from Doullens R.O.O.	
	26 March		Visited by A.D.O.S 6 Corps, who gave instructions that all surplus stores to be disposed of in the event of a hurried move. Orders to move at once to Warlus. Had one lorry only & this was commandeered by DHQ to remove their papers. I afterwards discovered that it had been utilised to carry away mess kit &c. Buried all M. Guns. Later the move was cancelled as the scare was false. Dug up guns. Move of 155 A. FA Bde from XIII Corps Troops to 31 Div. Indent on Rouen for 1000 dressings field – urgently required.	
	27	–	Contents of Div Armrs Shop & all surplus stores returned to base under A.D.O.S instructions. Also destroyed all documents over 2 months old. Indent for 10 Vickers Guns & mountings & 68 boxes belt Ammn for 31 M.G Battn to replace destroyed by shell fire.	
	28	–	Moved into Village from Camp & took over stores of O.O 6 Corps Troops. Had requests from several units to supply immediate needs. Did this where possible, the units were not being administered by me. Asked Corps whether I might form a small dump at railhead, so that if suddenly moved, stores could be dispatched by rail to base. Wired reply not to be done.	

A5834 Wt. W4973/M687 750,000 8/16 D. D. & L. Ltd. Forms/C.2118/13.

Army Form C. 2118.

Instructions regarding War Diaries and Intelligence Summaries are contained in F. S. Regs., Part II. and the Staff Manual respectively. Title pages will be prepared in manuscript.

WAR DIARY
or
~~INTELLIGENCE SUMMARY.~~

(Erase heading not required.)

Place	Date	Hour	Summary of Events and Information	Remarks and references to Appendices
Humbercamp	28/3		Move wire 0574 for 11 MG Squadron from unknown formation to this Div. 10 Vickers guns received + issued. Indent 0576 for 4.5 Carr. for D/165 to replace 62169 condemned wear. Wire from 6 Corps instructing DADOS to indent for one 18 pr. for A/155 AFA to replace 1248 destroyed shell fire. Indent submitted, came wire giving instructions that this would be moved to Gds. ~~[illegible]~~ Divn. ~~[illegible]~~ Ord 6 Corps asked to supply 10000 prs socks. 5000 only available. Issued on distribution made by 'Q'. OO. 6 C troops asked to supply flannelette – Nil available. Wire 0581 moving 34th ~~Div~~ Arty to this Divn: [illegible] move of 155 AFA Bde from 31st to Guards Div. Indent for 2nd Lewis gun Mags. for 92 Inf Bde. to replace destroyed shell fire. Received & issued. Indent for 2 Lewis guns for 4 Grenadiers to replace lost: & one for ~~4~~ for 11 E. Yorks to replace lost or destroyed in action. Ord Rouen wired to dispatch Dressings field per AMFO. as they could not send them per truck.	
	March 29.		Indent for Wagon GS for 123 Section DAC to replace one abandoned. Indent for 34 Div Arty, 18pr. springs RO. Issue 1st Order 2nd. Authority phoned from Corps. " " 13 Vickers Barrels to replace lost, destroyed & worn out. Wired Havre that others could not be accepted on indents of today's & following dates. Similar wire to Rouen. Indents for 15 Lewis guns for 10 & 11 E Yorks & 11 E Lancs. 4.5 & 6 respectively to replace lost destroyed by shell fire. Also for 774 Maps. & 244 Carriers maps. 2 L.G. for 13 Y & L to replace destroyed by shell fire.	
	Mar 30		Indent for 6 L.G. for 18 DLI to replace worn. Wire to 31 M.G Batt to draw 7 wagons L GS [illegible] from [illegible] Wire for 19 Lewis guns (including 3 AA) for 15 West Yorks to replace lost in action.	

Instructions regarding War Diaries and Intelligence Summaries are contained in F. S. Regs., Part II. and the Staff Manual respectively. Title pages will be prepared in manuscript.

WAR DIARY

or

~~INTELLIGENCE SUMMARY.~~

(Erase heading not required.)

Army Form C. 2118.

Place	Date	Hour	Summary of Events and Information	Remarks and references to Appendices
Humbercamps	30/3		Indent for one wagon telephone, one cart Maltese to 31 Div Sigs to replace damaged shell fire	
			" " one 18 pdr limber & carriage & one wagon Ammn. for A 165 Bde RFA to replace lost	
			Received wire from DOS requiring an estimate for Lewis Guns, Vickers & 3" Stokes	
	31/3		Received orders to move on April 1st to Lucheux.	
			Wired DOS an estimate which I obtained through 'Q'. (see 30th)	
			This is being written under adverse circumstances, in a barn shed & letting in the wet so that the blots on several of the pages are unavoidable. The men have worked hard & borne certain discomforts smilingly & I am proud to testify these facts.	
			W. J. Swallow Lieut for D.A.D.O.S. 31 Div 31/3/18	

A5834 Wt. W4973/M687 750,000 8/16 D. D. & L. Ltd. Forms/C.2118/13.

Army Form C. 2118.

DADOS 31 D
Vol 26

Instructions regarding War Diaries and Intelligence Summaries are contained in F. S. Regs., Part II. and the Staff Manual respectively. Title pages will be prepared in manuscript.

WAR DIARY
or
~~INTELLIGENCE SUMMARY~~.
(Erase heading not required.)

Place	Date	Hour	Summary of Events and Information	Remarks and references to Appendices
Humbercamp	1st April '18		Left for Lucheux. All stores in hand were accommodated in the four lorries. Did not offload	
Lucheux	2nd		Moved to Tinques & took over former dump – a poor place from both Ordnance & Units' points of view. Indents for 19 Lewis guns for 15th West Yorks (lost in action) 6 for 18 DLI to replace W/S 2 for 170 Bde RFA (shell fire)	
Tinques	3rd		RTO Tinques instructed to reconsign truck 24517 from Havre with Wagon G.S. for D 160 Bde. RFA. 31 DHQ to compile a Return (8099 (QC1)) d. 30.3.18 to clear up gun situation. Indent for 1 [illegible] for 13 Y.L. to replace lost in action. RTO Tinques instructed that if 12 trench mortars arrive they are to be reconsigned to Ordnance 32 Div.	
	4th		Indent for 1056 Rifle Grenade Dischargers No 36 under GRO 3440. 7 Lewis guns from under [illegible] for 11 E Yorks to replace lost through shell fire + 3 for 11 E Lancs for same reason. 4 Lewis guns for 13 Y & L to replace condemned by armourer 2 for 3rd Coldstream Gds to replace lost in action. RTO Mt St Eloi instructed to reconsign truck 26259 with 12 trench mortars to Ord 32 Div.	
	5th		Move notice to all concerned transferring HQ 34 Div Train to 31 Div on 28 [illegible], moving them back on 1st inst. Letter from GOC 3rd Army expressing his appreciation of the fine work done by the 31 Div in battles near Arras	
	6th		Move notice to all concerned transferring 31 Div Arty, DAC (HQ) + No 1 + 2 Sections DAC from 31 to 32 Div. Dados 31 suggested administering 31 Div Arty – 13th Corps agreed but 6th did not. Chief clerk in hospital. Bde Ord + storeman sent to Ord 32 to administer 31 D. Arty. [illegible] retained as my Chief Clerk in hospital.	
	7th		Proceeded with refitting. Calais base very prompt in dispatching stores.	
On the road near Hazebrouck	8th – 10th		Proceeded with refitting. Stopped on road outside Hazebrouck & reported to DHQ at La Motte. Ordered to move to Steenbecque. Ordered to move to Staple. Stopped on road outside Hazebrouck & reported to DHQ at La Motte. Ordered to stop where I was until further orders. Came under XV Corps + 57 Div Arty moved to 31 Div by HQ [illegible].	
	11th		This unit in a bad state evidently from the amount of stores required to bring them up to Mob. Establishment.	
Morbecque + Wallon Cappell	12th		Instructed to go to Morbecque. In the evening moved to Wallon Cappell. Just cleared Railhead – about 1½ tons of stores – + carted the lot to Wallon Cappell. No accommodation provided, so formed a dump on roadside. Soon as Div HQ moved from here, Dados secured a commodious barn, + could carry on his work in a more satisfactory manner under the improved conditions.	

Instructions regarding War Diaries and Intelligence Summaries are contained in F. S. Regs., Part II. and the Staff Manual respectively. Title pages will be prepared in manuscript.

WAR DIARY
or
~~INTELLIGENCE SUMMARY.~~
(Erase heading not required.)

Army Form C. 2118.

Place	Date	Hour	Summary of Events and Information	Remarks and references to Appendices
Hallow Capbell	13th April		15 Lewis Guns from Est No 1:- 2 for 10th Yorks, 4 to 11 E Yorks, 9 to 11 Cfamers. Indent for 6 Vickers Guns for 31 MGB to replace lost. All guns indented for were obtained within a few hours of receiving indents & issued immediately.	
			4 15 pdr limber wagons, 3 18 pdr Amm. wagons, 3 wagons G.S. for No 1 Sect DAC (57) to replace lost.	
	14		Instructed ROO Arme to return 4 trucks to Base as it was quite impossible to accept them, as my dump was so exposed & inadequate.	
			7 15 pdr Amm wagons, 7 18 pdr limber wagons, 5 wagons G.S. for No 2 Section 57 DAC.	
			16 Lewis Guns for 13 Y Hamers with spare parts etc. to replace lost.	
			1 wagon G.S. for No 1 Coy 57 Div. Train. 1 Lewis Gun for B/286 RFA (57th Div) to replace lost	
			16 Lewis guns to replace lost (complete with spare parts) for 18 DLI	
			12 " " " " " " " 4 Grenadier Gds	
			2 Vickers Guns " " " 31 M.G. Btn.	
			2nd Blanket to be returned as soon as possible.	
	15		19 L. Guns complete with spare parts to replace lost in action for 15 W. Yorks	
			" " " " " " 2 Irish Gds	
			12 " " " " " " "	
			1 Cart water tank " " " 12 KOYLI	
			3 Lewis Guns " " " "	
			7 wagons Amm. 18 pdr 2 limber wagon 18 pr for A/285 Bde RFA to replace lost in action	
			16 Lewis guns with spare parts etc etc " 11th E Yorks " " "	
			12 Vickers " " 31 M.G.B " " "	
			17 Mk II Vickers Barrels, 14 Oxford Mtgs. " " " " " "	
			25 Boxes spare parts, 6 Rods cleaning	

Army Form C. 2118.

Instructions regarding War Diaries and Intelligence Summaries are contained in F. S. Regs., Part II. and the Staff Manual respectively. Title pages will be prepared in manuscript.

WAR DIARY
or
~~INTELLIGENCE SUMMARY~~.
(Erase heading not required.)

Place	Date	Hour	Summary of Events and Information	Remarks and references to Appendices
Wallon Cappel	15th		Wired to Staff Capt 57 Divn to collect from Hazebrouck 4 18prs + limbers for 286 Bde RFA	
			17 Lewis Guns, Bags spare parts filled, Rods jointed + cleaning tools for 3rd Coldstream Gds to replace lost	
			2 18pr limber carriages for B/286 Bde RFA.	
			1 4.5 " " D/286 "	
	16th		Bader proceeded to Calais with two lorries to draw my clothing etc which was urgently required.	
			13 trucks advised at Arques railhead to be immediately cleared. With the assistance of 8 Motor lorries obtained through DAQMG this was done.	
			4 Lewis Guns to replace lost for 10 E Yorks.	
			6 18pr limbers wagons 2 wagons Ammn 18pr for B/286 Bde RFA. } To replace lost	
			2 4.5 limber carriages D/286 " " }	
			2 Lewis Guns complete for 10 E Yorks	
			1 Wagon G.S. 2 Section 57 DAC "	
			5 Lewis Guns, + 8 bags tools 4 Grenadier Gds "	
			Asked XV Corps for authority to draw [illegible] Signal pistols (Very) from [illegible] Park	
	17th		1 Cart Officers Mess for B/286 to replace lost	
	18th		384 Belts Ammn for 31 M.G.C. to complete to scale. Auth QMG. 8003/35. Q.C.T. of 16th inst	
			5 Vickers Guns for 31 M.G.B. to replace lost.	
			1 Cart Off. Mess to replace lost for A/285 Bde RFA	
			1 Cart Water Tank " " " 18 DLI.	
			1 Wagon limbered RE. (fore portion) 31 Divn Signals to replace one damaged by Shell fire	
	19th		1 Cart Officers Mess to replace lost for B/285 Bde RFA.	

A5834 Wt. W4973/M687 750,000 8/16 D. D. & L. Ltd. Forms/C.2118/13.

Instructions regarding War Diaries and Intelligence Summaries are contained in F. S. Regs., Part II. and the Staff Manual respectively. Title pages will be prepared in manuscript.

WAR DIARY
or
~~INTELLIGENCE~~ SUMMARY.
(*Erase heading not required.*)

Army Form C. 2118.

Place	Date	Hour	Summary of Events and Information	Remarks and references to Appendices
Wallon Cappel	20th		1 Breech Mech^m for D/285 to replace.	
	22nd		Move of Lewis Gun Bttn of 4 Tank Bde. to 31 Div from another formation	
	23rd		Indent for clip on jackets for box respirators to Equip Division	
			1 Wagon limbered R.E. body for 31 Div Signals to replace lost.	
			1 18 pdr limber carriage for C/285 Bde R.F.A. } to replace lost.	
			3 " " Wagon Ammn " "	
			1 4.5 Wagon Ammn for D/286 "	
	24th		6 4.5 Wagons Ammn } D/485 to replace lost	
			6 4.5 limbers	
			1 Vickers Gun to replace destroyed shell fire for 31. M.G. Bttn. Dados went to No 6 Park to obtain it at once	
			1 Car Maltese for 31 M.G. Bttn ———	
			1 18 pdr limber carriage } for A/286 ———	
	25th		1 AA Lewis Gun for D/286 to replace lost	
			2 AA " for C/286 " "	
			1 Wagon G.S. No 2 Sec DAC "	
	27		1 Pontoon Bipartite for 431 Field Coy R.E. to replace condemned.	
Hondeghem	28		Moved to Hondeghem & provided with decent accommodation for stores.	

Army Form C. 2118.

Instructions regarding War Diaries and Intelligence Summaries are contained in F. S. Regs., Part II. and the Staff Manual respectively. Title pages will be prepared in manuscript.

WAR DIARY
or
~~INTELLIGENCE SUMMARY.~~
(Erase heading not required.)

Place	Date	Hour	Summary of Events and Information	Remarks and references to Appendices
Hondeghem	30		4 Lewis Guns to complete 12 KOYLI to scale of 12 under QMG 8003/14. QC1. 25/4/18 Instructed No 3 Section 31 DAC & No 1 Sec 57 DAC to draw each one wagon G S from Canadian reserve park As will be seen the 57 Div Artillery have required a great deal of attention as so much of their equipment was lost. A S Swallow DADOS 31 Div 1/5/18	

A5834 Wt. W4973/M687 750,000 8/16 D. D. & L. Ltd. Forms/C.2118/13.

Confidential Volume XXIX

Vol 27

War Diary.

D.A.D.O.S.

31st Divn.

May. 1918.

Instructions regarding War Diaries and Intelligence Summaries are contained in F. S. Regs., Part II. and the Staff Manual respectively. Title pages will be prepared in manuscript.

Army Form C. 2118.

WAR DIARY
or
~~INTELLIGENCE SUMMARY.~~
(Erase heading not required.)

Place	Date	Hour	Summary of Events and Information	Remarks and references to Appendices
Hondeghem	May 2		Indent O.935 for one Kitchen Travelling body for 13 Y+L to replace condemned.	
			" O 945 - one hot water Tank for 12 KOYLI. " "	
	4		" O 946 - one Rear portion Wagon Lim. G.S. for 13 Y+L to replace condemned.	
			Cond. Major [illegible] joined Ordnance as Chief Clerk vice Cond. [illegible] who went sick at [illegible]. Reconstruction of [illegible] clothing commenced. Arrangements made with [illegible]	
	5		One Wagon G.S. surplus in 31 Bn. MG Coy supplied to 31 DAC to meet demand	
	6		Indent O 954 for two Mk I barrels for X/TMB (57 Div) to replace lost.	
			" O 955 three " " " Y/TMB (57 Div) "	
	8		Move Wire O 962 of 57 Div Arty from 31 to 57 Div.	
			Indent O 964 for one fore portion of Wagon limbered G.S. for 13 Y+L to replace condemned	
	13		Indent O 980 for 36 Lewis Guns to complete 31 Div. to Scale "D" Auth.y 15 Corps Wire H.O 538 of 13th inst.	
	14		A Driver 223 Field Coy R.E. killed in Store yard by A.A. Shell case.	
	15		The 36 Lewis Guns demanded on 13th received + issued to units.	
	16		Indent O 985 for 70 Sprayers for fly-killing solution under Authority 2nd Army Q.O.4 205/1/1 12 5/18.	
	17		Indent O 988 for one fore portion of wagon limbered G.S. for 13 Y+L to replace condemned	

A5834 Wt. W4973/M687 750,000 8/16 D. D. & L. Ltd. Forms/C.2118/13.

Instructions regarding War Diaries and Intelligence Summaries are contained in F. S. Regs., Part II. and the Staff Manual respectively. Title pages will be prepared in manuscript.

WAR DIARY

or

~~INTELLIGENCE SUMMARY.~~

(Erase heading not required.)

Army Form C. 2118.

Place	Date	Hour	Summary of Events and Information	Remarks and references to Appendices
Hondeghem	19		DADOS XV Corps informed by memo O.990 that all important articles of winter clothing had been returned.	
			Indent O991 for 31 mountings for Lewis Guns (A.A) as a first supply under authority 2nd Army Q.O. 11/156 of 2nd inst.	
	20		Move of 4th Gds Brigade including their TMB from 31 Div. to XIX Corps. Attd to Guard's Division. Necessary notices despatched re transfer of Indents	
	22		Bomb dropped by enemy Aircraft in field outside Office. Two H.Q. Clerks wounded.	
	23		Divisional Commander sent a letter congratulating the Ordnance on their good work re Equipping 57 Div Arty.	
Blaringhem	24		Moved to Blaringhem, taking over Office & Dump vacated by Ordnance IX Division.	
			Indent O1003 for two Stokes Mortars, to replace condemned for 92 TMB	
			Received notice of my appointment as DADOS of 31 Division as from April 23rd.	
	26		431 Field Coy RE moved from 31 Div to 59 Div. Corps informed that 1070 sleeve jackets had been returned to Base	
	28.		Inspected Q.M. Stores of 92 Brigade in accordance with G.R.O. 3556.	
	30		" " " " 93 " " " " "	
			The Diary this month apart from Departmental work is not of much interest. The Division is almost fully equipped according to Mob. Stores Tables with the exception of a few items that are on the shortage list	
			W. Swallow Captain DADOS 31 Division	

197

DADOS 31 D
~~41 Mob Vety~~
Vol 28

Instructions regarding War Diaries and Intelligence Summaries are contained in F. S. Regs., Part II. and the Staff Manual respectively. Title pages will be prepared in manuscript.

WAR DIARY
~~or~~
~~INTELLIGENCE SUMMARY.~~
(Erase heading not required.)

Army Form C. 2118.

Place	Date	Hour	Summary of Events and Information	Remarks and references to Appendices
BLARINGHEM	June			
	1		Two Stokes Mortars received for 92 T.M.B. Indents for 1 Lewis Gun to replace condemned for 15 West Yorks + 1 Cartwater Tank for 10 E. Yorks. DADOS visited Q. Master 93rd Bgde + inspected their stores	
	2		Arrival of Headquarters of New Brigade (94th.). Visited Q. Master of 92nd Brigade + inspected stores	
	3		Indent for 1 Cat Officers Mess for 12 K.O.Y.L.I. to replace condemned. Inspected Q.M Stores of K.O.Y.L.I.	
	4		DADOS granted leave from 4th – 19th.	
	5.		Indent for 8 Stokes Mortars complete – a first issue – for 94 T.M.B.	
			Indent for 120 Lewis Guns to complete Infantry Battalions to scale G. Authority 2nd Army G 266.	
	7		Ordnance VI Corps advised of departure of Clerk + Storeman from 31 Divn for duty with first Divn	
			Indent for 4 Lewis Guns A.A. as a first supply to 2nd L.N. Lancs.	
			Indent for one Kitchen travelling body for 11 E. Yorks to replace condemned.	
			Received the 8 Trench Mortars for 94 T.M.B + 124 Lewis Guns for 94th Brigade	
			Indent for 3000 H.C Containers for Box Respirators – 1st supply – for units from overseas.	
	9.		Indent for Wagons Limbered G.S. fore – one, rear – one, to replace condemned for 12 K.O.Y.L.I.	
			" " " " " " 1 " 2 "	2 L.N.L
	10		" for 4 Lewis Guns A.A. (First supply) for 2 R. M. Fusiliers.	
	11.		Indent for 6000 Cartridges Dummy Drill.	
			" " Kitchen travelling body one for 11 E. Yorks To replace Condemned	

A5834 Wt. W4973/M687 750,000 8/16 D. D. & L. Ltd. Forms/C.2118/13.

Instructions regarding War Diaries and Intelligence Summaries are contained in F. S. Regs., Part II. and the Staff Manual respectively. Title pages will be prepared in manuscript.

WAR DIARY
or
~~INTELLIGENCE SUMMARY.~~
(Erase heading not required.)

Army Form C. 2118.

Place	Date	Hour	Summary of Events and Information	Remarks and references to Appendices
Blaringhem	June 12		Ordnance Gun Park asked if post mountings for Lewis Guns A.A. were available. Answer in the negative	
	13.		Indent for 4 Lewis Guns A A for 2 R Dublin Fusiliers	
	15.		Indent for one Wagon G.S. for 12. K.O.Y.L.I. to replace condemned.	
			" " 12 Rampole racks for carrying Lewis Guns in Limbers without boxes. Authority D.O.S. O.S.A. 3/110 dated 14-6-18	
	17.		2nd Dublin Fusiliers + 2nd Munster Fusiliers moved from 31 Divn to O.D. Dieppe	
			Received 4 AA Gun Lewis for R. Dublin Fusiliers	
	20.		"Q" informed D.A.D.O.S that he had been made a Major.	
	21.		Indent one Wagon Limb. G.S. to replace condemned for 12 KOYLI	
WALLON CAPELL.	22		Moved from Blaringhem to Wallon Capell. Took over Dump of 29th Division	
			2nd Loyal North Lancs moved from 31st Division to 34th Division.	
	23.		Indent for one ~~Lewis~~ Gun Vickers for 31 M.G.B. to replace one destroyed Shell fire	
	24.		Gun Vickers for 31 M.G.B received.	
	25.		Indent for 7 Guns Lewis to replace damaged by shell fire for 11 E. Lancs	
	27.		7 Guns Lewis received for 11 E. Lancs + indent for one rear portion of Wagon Limbd G.S. for No.3. Section 31 D.A.C. to replace condemned.	
	30.		Indent for 12 Bed beds for 6" Newton Trench Mortars as a 1st Supply under G.R.O 3826 for X + Y 31 T.M.B.	
			Indent for one Wagon G.S. to replace condemned for No 1 Section 31 DAC.	

W.S. Waller Major
DADOS 31 Divn
30.6.18

A5834 Wt. W4973/M687 750,000 8/16 D. D. & L. Ltd. Forms/C.2118/13.

Army Form C. 2118.

Instructions regarding War Diaries and Intelligence Summaries are contained in F. S. Regs., Part II. and the Staff Manual respectively. Title pages will be prepared in manuscript.

WAR DIARY
or
~~INTELLIGENCE SUMMARY.~~
(Erase heading not required.)

(1) Dawos 31 D
Vol 29

Place	Date	Hour	Summary of Events and Information	Remarks and references to Appendices
WALLON CAPPEL	July 1		Indent 0/1115 for one Lewis Gun for 10 E Yorks to replace condemned	
			" 0/1116 - one fore portion wagon limb G.S. 11 E. Lancs to replace condemned.	
			" 0/1117 - one Lewis Gun for 18 D.L.I. to replace destroyed shell fire.	
	2		" 0/1119 - four Lewis Guns for 11 E Lancs to replace condemned.	
			" 0/1120 - One Kitchen travelling Body for 15 W Yorks to replace condemned.	
			" 0/1121 - One Wagon G.S. for 211 Field Co R.E. " "	
	3		" 0/1122 - one Lewis Gun for 13 York & Lancs to replace destroyed shellfire	
	4		" 0/1125 - one Stokes barrel to replace destroyed shell fire 92 T.M.B.	
			" 0/1126 - one Wagon G.S. for 12 KOYLI to replace condemned	
			" 0/1128 - one 18 pdr. to replace 6908 - Serving - for A165 Bde R.F.A.	
			" 0/1129 - one K. Travelling body for 13 York & Lancs to replace condemned.	
	6		" 0/1132 - one Kitchen Trolley ~~body~~ complete for 31st Battn M.G.B	
	7		Received off Indent 0/1128 7th inst. one 18 pdr. No 9773.	
	8		Indent 0/1186 for one Vickers Gun complete for instructional purposes for 31 Bn M.G.B. Authority 2nd Army Q.O. 4/255/1/1 of 6th inst.	
			" 0/1138 for two Lewis Guns for 15 W Yorks to replace lost.	

A5834 Wt. W4973/M687 750,000 8/16 D. D. & L. Ltd. Forms/C.2118/13.

WAR DIARY
or
~~INTELLIGENCE SUMMARY.~~
(Erase heading not required.)

Instructions regarding War Diaries and Intelligence Summaries are contained in F. S. Regs., Part II. and the Staff Manual respectively. Title pages will be prepared in manuscript.

Army Form C. 2118.

(2)

Place	Date	Hour	Summary of Events and Information	Remarks and references to Appendices
WALLON CAPPEL	JULY 10		Indent O/1139 for one fore portion wagon Limber G.S. for S.A.A. Section D.A.C. to replace condemned.	
	12		Indent O/1142 for one Kitchen Travelling body for 13 York + Lancs to replace condemned.	
	13		Indent O/1144 for one Stokes Mortar for 92 T.M.B. to replace condemned.	
	14.		Indent O/1146 for 12 Lewis Guns for 210. 211. 223 Fd Coys R.E. (Auth G.H.Q. letter O.B. 1213. 2.7.18. One Stokes Mortar received off indent O/1144 of 13th inst.	
	15.		Indent O 1149 for one wagon Limbered R.E. for 223 Field Coy to replace condemned.	
	16.		Indent O 1151 for one rear portion of wagon Limb. G.S. for 13 York + Lancs to replace condemned.	
	17.		12 Lewis Guns received off Indent O/1146 for the Field Coys 210. 211. 223.	
	18.		Indent O/1154 for 16 Lewis Guns complete for 165 + 170 Bdes R.F.A. to complete to scale under GHQ letter O.B. 1315 of 16.7.18. Armourers' Shop (Divisional) reopened.	
	19.		Indent O/1157 for one wagon Limb. G.S. complete for 31 D. Signal Co. to replace condemned.	
			" O/1158 for one Kitchen Travelling body for 12 R.S.F. to replace condemned.	
			" O/1159 for one wagon G.S. for No. 1 Sect D.A.C. to replace condemned.	
			D.A.D.O.S. proceeded to XV Corps Officers' Rest Hostel for 1 week. S	
	20.		Ordnance XV Corps informed 24 Mats Guns No 2 to complete Batteries to 2 per gun. Their O.S. 1453 of 20/7	
	21.		Indent O/1163 for one Vickers Gun for 31 M.G. Batt. to replace destroyed. 16 Lewis Guns received off Indent O/1154 of 18 inst. Indent O/1165 for one Lewis Gun for 10 E. Yorks to replace condemned	

A5834 Wt. W4973/M687 750,000 8/16 D. D. & L. Ltd. Forms/C.2118/13.

Instructions regarding War Diaries and Intelligence Summaries are contained in F. S. Regs., Part II. and the Staff Manual respectively. Title pages will be prepared in manuscript.

WAR DIARY
or
~~INTELLIGENCE SUMMARY.~~
(Erase heading not required.)

(3)

Army Form C. 2118.

Place	Date	Hour	Summary of Events and Information	Remarks and references to Appendices
WALLON CAPPEL	July 22		Indent O/1167 for one Cart Officers' Mess to replace condemned for C/170. Bde R.F.A.	
	23		Lewis Guns received off indents O/1162 of 20 + O/1165 of 21 inst. Also Vickers Gun off O/1163 of 21 inst.	
	24.		Indent O/1173 for one Wagon Pontoon for 211 Field Coy RE to replace condemned.	
	25		Indent O/1174 for 3 Lewis Guns Complete for 18 DLI to replace lost.	
			O/1175 2 " " for 12 R.S. Fusiliers " "	
	26.		Indent O/1176 for one Kitchen Travelling Body for 2/4 R.W. Fusiliers to replace condemned	
	27		DADOS returned to duty from Rest Hostel.	
	29.		XV Corps ADOS informed in reply to his wire OS 1508 of even date that 99 revolvers were due out.	
	30.		Lewis Guns received off Indents O/1174 + O/1175 of 25th inst.	
			Indent O/1181 for one Lewis Gun for 12 Norfolks to replace Condemned	
			" O/1182 - six " " to replace lost for 15 W Yorks.	
	31.		Indent O/1184 for one Wagon GS to replace condemned for No 2 Sec. DAC	
			Indent O/1186 for one Lewis Gun for 31 M.G. Batt - to replace destroyed Shellfire	
			Lewis Guns received off indents O/1181/1182 of 30th inst	
			1-8-18	
			[signature] Major DADOS 31 Div.	

A5834 Wt. W4973/M687 750,000 8/16 D. D. & L. Ltd. Forms/C.2118/13.

Instructions regarding War Diaries and Intelligence Summaries are contained in F. S. Regs., Part II. and the Staff Manual respectively. Title pages will be prepared in manuscript.

WAR DIARY
or
~~INTELLIGENCE SUMMARY.~~
(Erase heading not required.)

Army Form C. 2118.

DADOS 31 D

VR 30

Place	Date	Hour	Summary of Events and Information	Remarks and references to Appendices
WALLON CAPELL	August 1		One Vickers Gun received off Indent 0/1186 of 31 ult for Machine Gun Coy. Visited units & Gun park No 2	
	2		Indent 0/1188 for one wagon G.S. to replace condemned for KOYLI (12th)	
			" 0/1189 " " " " " " " No 2 Sec DAC.	
	3		" 0/1192 " " " Limbered RE " " " 223 Field Coy.	
	4		" 0/1193 " one Lewis Gun for 12 R Scots F. to replace condemned.	
	5		" 0/1194 " one wagon limb G.S. to replace condemned for 10 E Yorks.	
			Lewis Gun received off indent 0/1193 of 4 inst.	
	6		Indent 0/1197 for one Stokes Mortar to replace condemned for 92 T.M.B. King George visited Wallon Capelle.	
	7		Indent 0/1198 for 1 Lewis Gun to replace destroyed by shellfire for 10 E Yorks	
			" 0/1199 " " " " " " " for 18 DLI.	
			One Stokes mortar received off indent 0/1197 of 6 instant.	
	8		Two Lewis Guns received off indents 0/1198 + 1199 of 7th inst. Meeting of Quartermasters	
	9		Indent 0/1207 for one cart Officers' Mess for A/165 to replace condemned.	
	10		Indent 0/1210 for one wagon limb G.S. to replace condemned for 13 Y+L.	
	13		Indent 0/1212 for one Kitchen Travelling Body to replace condemned for 11 E. Yorks	
			" 0/1213 for one 4·5" How without B.C.M. to replace condemned for wear for D 165	

A5834 Wt. W4973/M687 750,000 8/16 D. D. & L. Ltd. Forms/C.2118/13.

Instructions regarding War Diaries and Intelligence Summaries are contained in F. S. Regs., Part II. and the Staff Manual respectively. Title pages will be prepared in manuscript.

WAR DIARY
or
~~INTELLIGENCE SUMMARY.~~
(*Erase heading not required.*)

Army Form C. 2118.

2

Place	Date	Hour	Summary of Events and Information	Remarks and references to Appendices
WALLON CAPELL	August 14		Visited units. Indent 0/1216 for 1 Stokes Mortar barrel for 92 T M B to replace one destroyed by premature. Received 4.5 How No 3942 off indent 0/1213 of 7th inst for D/165.	
	15		Question of wagon repairs done in the field. Corps informed no records kept, but approximately 100 wagons (chiefly G.S.) repaired during June & July. Received Stokes barrel off indent 0/1216 of 14th inst.	
	16		Indent 0.1225 for 1 18 pdr with Bcy to replace No 4720 Condemned for C/165	
	17		18 pdr received of Indent 0/1225 of 16th.	
	18		Indent 0/1229 for one Lewis Gun tunnel & bags S.P. filled to replace destroyed Shell fire for 12 Norfolks	
	19		Received 1 Lewis Gun off Indent 0.1229 of 18th	
	21		Ordnance 2nd Army asked for authority to draw 60 racks for carrying water. Urgently required. Authority received & racks drawn.	
	22		Indent 0/1233 for 1 18 pdr with Bcy to replace No 8260 - scoring - for A/165 Visited Hondeghem	
HONDEGHEM	24		Moved to Hondeghem. Work over dump & located as in April last. Indent 0.1237 for one 18 pdr to replace 4782 - inaccurate - for B/170 Auth. Q M G 8055 (Q.O.1) d/ 22/8	
	26		18 pdr received off indent 0.1237. Gun No. 2207. Indent 0.1240 for 18 pdr with Bm to replace No 5258 - scoring - for B/170	
	28		18 pdr No. 8477 received off Indent 0.1240 of 26 inst. Indent 0.1242 for 1 18 pdr with Bm, to replace 3672 - Scoring - for C/165 " 0.1243 " " " " - without " " " " 5420 - " - " C/170	

A5834 Wt. W4973/M687 750,000 8/16 D. D. & L. Ltd. Forms/C.2118/13.

Instructions regarding War Diaries and Intelligence Summaries are contained in F. S. Regs., Part II. and the Staff Manual respectively. Title pages will be prepared in manuscript.

WAR DIARY
or
INTELLIGENCE SUMMARY.
(Erase heading not required.)

Army Form C. 2118.

3

Place	Date	Hour	Summary of Events and Information	Remarks and references to Appendices
HONDEGHEM	August 29		Indent O.1244 for 1 Lewis Gun + 7 bags spare parts to replace destroyed shell fire for 12 Norfolks.	
			Indent O.1245 – 1 Kitchen Trav Body to replace condemned for 11 E Lancs	
			Indent O.1246 – 1 Lewis Gun to replace condemned for 12 Norfolks	
			18pdrs Nos. 6419 + 265 received off indents O.1242/3 of 28th inst.	
	30		Indent O.1248 for one Lewis Gun to replace destroyed by shell fire for 13 Y&L.	
			Lewis Gun received off indents O.1244/6 of 29th inst.	
			Indent O.1250 for one 18pdr and Body to replace No 7218 (scoring) for A/170	
	31		Ordnance XV Corps asked to obtain authority from Army for 50 sets pack saddlery urgently required	
			18pdr No. 9564 received off indent O.1250 of 30 inst.	
			Indent O.1253 for 1 4.5 How. and Body to replace 1522 – wear – for D/165.	
			DADOS visited most of the units during the month, as well as the Gun Park No 2. the different dumps.	
			[signature] Major DADOS 31 Div. 1 – 9 – 18	

A5834 Wt. W4973/M687 750,000 8/16 D. D. & L. Ltd. Forms/C.2118/13.

Instructions regarding War Diaries and Intelligence Summaries are contained in F. S. Regs., Part II. and the Staff Manual respectively. Title pages will be prepared in manuscript.

WAR DIARY
or
~~INTELLIGENCE~~ SUMMARY.

(*Erase heading not required.*)

Army Form C. 2118.

(1) DADOS 31 D

WO 95/2350 [?] 31

Place	Date	Hour	Summary of Events and Information	Remarks and references to Appendices
Hondeghem	1st Sept '18		Visited Caestre to arrange new Dump & office. Indent O.1255 for wagon G.S. to replace condemned for No. 3 Section 31 DAC. One 4.5 How. No. 3509 received off indent O.1253 of 31 ult.	
Caestre	2.		Moved to Caestre. Indent O 1257 for 1 18pdr without B.M. to replace No. 1204 condemned for scoring for A/165 Bde. Indent O 1528 for 2 Lewis Guns & spare parts filled for 11 East Lancs	
	3		Lewis Guns off O.1528 received	
	4		Indent O 1263 for 1 wagon cable limbered for 31 Div Signal Co. R.E. 18 pdr No 2743 received off indent O.1257.	
	5.		Indent O 1265 for one wagon G.S. for No 1 Sec DAC. Ord XV Corps informed in reply to their O.S.1704 that NIL sights A.A. & 4 mountings A.A. required to complete. Indent No 1268 for one 4.5 How without B.M. to replace No. 1136 - scored chamber - for D/165 Bde.	
	7		Indent O.1271 for 5 Lewis Guns to replace lost for 11 E LANCS " O 1272 " 3 " " " " Shellfire - 10 E YORKS " O 1273 " 2 Vickers " " " " for 31 M.G.C.	
	8.		Guns off indents of 7th inst received. Indent O/1276 for 1 18pdr. and B.M. to replace No 2680 for scoring B/165 Bde.	
	9.		One 4.5 How received off indent O/1278 of 5th. Indent O/1280 for 2 water carts for 12 Norfolk Regt to replace condemned. Indent O/1281 for one 18 pdr. with B.M. to replace No 8069 - scoring - for C/165 Bde " O/1282 for 6 Lewis Guns & Gun Stores for 10 E. YORKS. to replace shell fire. One 18 pdr received off indent O/[illegible] [illegible]	
	10.		One 18 pdr. No. 5929 received off indent O/1281 of 9th inst.	
	11.		Indent O/1287 for one 18pdr. without B.M. to replace No 659 scoring for C/170 Bde.	

Instructions regarding War Diaries and Intelligence Summaries are contained in F. S. Regs., Part II. and the Staff Manual respectively. Title pages will be prepared in manuscript.

WAR DIARY
or
~~INTELLIGENCE SUMMARY.~~
(Erase heading not required.)

Army Form C. 2118.

(2)

Place	Date	Hour	Summary of Events and Information	Remarks and references to Appendices
Caestre	Sept.	13th	Nos. 227 + 224 Field Coy R.E. moved to me for administration from Ordnance X Corps Troops.	
			18pdr No 9060 received off indent 0/1287 of 11th. Indent 0/1293 for Wagon pontoons to replace condemned for 211 Field Co.	
		14	Indent 0/1295 for 18000 blankets G.S. as first supply under authority Q.M.G. 4041. (Q.B.1)	
			0/1297 Indent for one wagon G.S. to replace condemned for C/165	
			Indent 0/1298 for one " G.S. " " " 24 R Welsh Fusiliers	
		15	Indent 0/1301 for one Cart water tank for 13 Y + LANCS to replace condemned.	
		16	ADOS XV Corps informed in reply to his O.S 1789 of 15th inst that Medium T.M. Bs. had no 6 Mortars	
			Indent 0/1304 for 2 Lewis Guns to replace Condemned for 12th NORFOLKS.	
			" 0/1305 - 1 Cart water tank " " " for 11th E YORKS.	
		17	2 Lewis Guns received off Indent 0/1304 of 16th.	
		18.	Indent 0/1309 for 8 Lewis Guns + various parts for 11 E. YORKS, to replace destroyed shell fire	
			" 0/1310 " 1 " " for 31 Div Reception Camp under G.R.O. 4954. Moved X+Y T.M. Batteries to II Corps Troops	
		19	Received Lewis Guns off Indents 0/1309 + 0/1310 of 18th inst. DADOS visited Gun Park, Dumps etc.	
		21.	Indent 0/1317 for one Vickers Gun for 31 M.G.C. to replace destroyed shell fire	
			" 0/1319 " 2 " " " " " "	
		22	Guns on indents of 21st received. Corps asked to obtain authority for Pack saddlery, [illegible] operations. Conference at Corps.	
		23	Indent 0/1326 for one Lewis Gun to replace destroyed shell fire for 15 West Yorks.	
		24	Indent 0/1331 for one 4'5 How with BM + Carriage to replace No 3509 + No 61970 respectively, destroyed by premature, for D 165 Bde. 2 Lewis Guns received off indents 0/1326 + 0/1328 of 23rd inst.	

Army Form C. 2118.

(3)

WAR DIARY
or
INTELLIGENCE SUMMARY.
(Erase heading not required.)

Instructions regarding War Diaries and Intelligence Summaries are contained in F. S. Regs., Part II. and the Staff Manual respectively. Title pages will be prepared in manuscript.

Place	Date	Hour	Summary of Events and Information	Remarks and references to Appendices
Caestre	25th Sept		Indent 0/1335 for one 18 pdr. without B.M. to replace No 7356 scoring, for A/170 Bde.	
			" 0/1336 " " " " " " No 6752 of A/165 withdrawn under authority Q.M.G. 8171 (Q.C.1)	
			" 0/1337 for 9 Hot Food Containers to complete to scale under G.R.O. 5074	
	26		One 18 pdr. No 1621 received off indent 0/1335 for A/170 + 18 pdr. No 556 off indent 0/1336 for A/165 and 4.5 How. No 3566 and Carriage No 13401 received off indents 0/1331 of 24th inst for D/165.	
			Indent 0/1339 for 1 18 pdr. without B.M. to replace No 7132 condemned scoring for C/165 Bde.	
			" 0/1341 for the 3" Stokes barrel to replace condemned for 94 T.M.B. Indent 0/1342 for [illegible] F.A.	
	27		Stokes barrel received off indent 0/1341 of 26th inst.	
	28		Indent 0/1344 for one Vickers gun complete for 31 M.G.B. to replace destroyed shell fire. Received [illegible]	
	29		18 pdr. No 1057 received off indent 0/1339 of 26th inst. Indent 0/1347 for one 18 pdr. without B.M. to replace No 5407 [illegible] scoring for A/170 Bde. Indent 0/1348 for one wagon G.S. to replace condemned for No 2 Sect. 31st D.A.C.	
			Indent 0/1349 for 500 bags for carrying rations to troops. Auth. D.D.O.S. O.S.G. 2040 of 30/10/17 + 2nd Army [illegible]	
	30		Indent 0/1360 for one Vickers gun barrel to replace condemned wear for 31 M.G.C.	
			18 pdr. No 4568 received off indent 0/1347 of 29th inst.	
			One Vickers " " " 0/1353 - 30th -	

[signature] Lt.Col. [illegible]
D.A.D.O.S. 31st Div.
2/x/18

A5834 Wt. W4973/M687 750,000 8/16 D. D. & L. Ltd. Forms/C.2118/13.

Instructions regarding War Diaries and Intelligence Summaries are contained in F. S. Regs., Part II. and the Staff Manual respectively. Title pages will be prepared in manuscript.

WAR DIARY
or
~~INTELLIGENCE SUMMARY.~~
(Erase heading not required.)

DADOS

Vol 32

Army Form C. 2118.

Place	Date	Hour	Summary of Events and Information	Remarks and references to Appendices
Caestre.	October 1.		Indent 0/1353 for one Vickers for 31 M G Coy to replace destroyed shell fire	
	2		" 0/1354 - one 18 pdr. without B.M. for B/165 Bde. to replace No 7229 Condemned scoring	
			" 0/1356 - " " " " - C/165 " " No 7095 " "	
			One Vickers gun received off Indent 0/1353 of 1st inst	
	3		Indent 0/1357 for one 18 pdr. without B.M. to replace No 7313 condemned scoring A/170 Bde.	
			" 0/1358 - " Vickers for 31 M G Coy to replace destroyed shell fire	
			18 pdrs No 1402, for C/165 + No 11258 for B/165 received off indents 0/1356 + 0/1354 of 2nd inst	
			One Vickers received off indent 0/1358 of today's date	
	4		18 pdr No 11030 received off indent 0/1357 of 3 inst.	
	5		Indent 0/1367 for 4 Lewis Guns to replace destroyed shell fire for 10 E Yorks. Received same day	
			" 0/1368 " 1 18 pdr without B.M. to replace No. 8208 condemned scoring for C/165 Bde	
			One Lewis Gun spare part wallet received for trial under A.D.O.S XV Corps O.S. 20/2/37 of 20th ult.	
			Indent 0/1371 for one Lewis Gun to replace destroyed shell fire for 18 D.L.I.	
	6		18 pdr No 10411 received off indent 0/1368 of 5th inst.	
	7		One Lewis Gun received off indent 0/1371 of 5th inst.	
			Indent 0/1374 for one 4.5" How for D/170 to replace No 1861 condemned wear.	
	8		4.5" Howitzer received off indent 0/1374 of 7th inst.	
	10		Indent 0/1377 for 10,000 blankets for 2nd issue	
			" 0/1379 " 3 Lewis Guns to replace destroyed shell fire for 15 West Yorks.	

A5834 Wt. W4973/M687 750,000 8/16 D. D. & L. Ltd. Forms/C.2118/13.

Instructions regarding War Diaries and Intelligence Summaries are contained in F. S. Regs., Part II. and the Staff Manual respectively. Title pages will be prepared in manuscript.

WAR DIARY
or
~~INTELLIGENCE SUMMARY.~~
(Erase heading not required.)

Army Form C. 2118.

2

Place	Date	Hour	Summary of Events and Information	Remarks and references to Appendices
Bacolme	11 Oct 16		Lewis Guns received off indent 0/1379 of 10th inst.	
La Crêche	12	-	Moved to La Crêche.	
			Indent 0/1383 for 1 4.5" How to replace No 57 condemned for wear for D/165 Bde.	
			" 0/1384 " 1 18pdr " " No 7915 " scoring " A/165 "	
			" 0/1385 " 2 18 pdrs " " No 1585 + 8299 " " " B/165 "	
	13	-	" 0/1387 " 1 18pdr " " No. 2610 " " " " C/170 "	
			" 0/1388 " 1 4.5 How. " " No. 210 condemned wear for D/170 "	
			Received 4.5 How No 2674 off indent 0/1383 for D/165	
			" 1 18pdr No 7145 " " 0/1384 " A/165	
			" 2 18pdr No 10436 + 5365 } off " 0/1385 " B/165	
			" 1 " No 10399 " " 0/1387 C/170	
	14	-	Indent 0/1391 for one wagon limbered G.S. for 31 Div Signal Coy.	
	15	-	Indent 0/1392 " 1 Vickers Gun to replace destroyed shell fire for 31 Batt. M.G.C.	
			" 0/1393 " 1 18pdr to replace No 7312 condemned scoring for A/165.	
			" 0/1394 for one wagon limbered G.S. hind portion for 134 [illegible] to replace condemned	
			Received 4.5 How 3759 off indent 0/1388 for D/170 Bde.	
	16		" one Vickers Gun off indent 0/1392 for 31 Machine Gun Batt.	
			" one 18 pdr off indent 0/1393 for A/165	

Instructions regarding War Diaries and Intelligence Summaries are contained in F. S. Regs., Part II. and the Staff Manual respectively. Title pages will be prepared in manuscript.

WAR DIARY
or
~~INTELLIGENCE SUMMARY.~~
(Erase heading not required.)

3

Army Form C. 2118.

Place	Date	Hour	Summary of Events and Information	Remarks and references to Appendices
La Crèche to Lannoy	Oct	21	Wired Base to postpone issue of 2nd blankets until after 24th. Moved to Lannoy.	
Lannoy		23	Indent 0/1405 Stores portion Wagon limbered G.S. for H.Q. 93 Inf Bde.	
		24	" 1 Wagon limbered G.S. complete for 31 Div Signals.	
		26	Indent 0/1409 Lewis Gun for 15 W. Yorks.	
			0/1408 Wagon limbered G.S. complete for 31 Div Signals	
Near Bavone		27	Moved to H.20 a.5.3 sheet 29. Transferred to II Corps. No 2 Anti Aircraft Coy & 227 Field Coy R.E. transferred to 2nd Army Troops N.3	
		30	Received one Lewis Gun of indent 0/1409 for 15 West Yorks.	
		31	Indent 3 Lewis Guns for 13 Y&Lancs. Issue 0/1424	

W.S. Swallow Major
DADOS 31 Div

A5834 Wt. W4973/M687 750,000 8/16 D. D. & L. Ltd. Forms/C.2118/13.

DADOS

Vol 33

Instructions regarding War Diaries and Intelligence Summaries are contained in F. S. Regs., Part II. and the Staff Manual respectively. Title pages will be prepared in manuscript.

WAR DIARY
or
INTELLIGENCE SUMMARY.
(Erase heading not required.)

Army Form C. 2118.

Place	Date	Hour	Summary of Events and Information	Remarks and references to Appendices
Near Courtrai Sheet 29 H 20 a 5.3	November 1		Received three Lewis Guns - 13 York & Lancs - off indent O/1424 dated 31.10.18.	
	2		234 Field Coy R.E. transferred from 31st Division to Ordnance Calais. Indent O/1429 for one wagon G.S. to replace condemned for 31st D.A.C. Indent O/1430 for one 18 pdr carriage without sights to replace 29890 for A/165 Bde. Received & issued to No 9 Ordnance Mobile Workshop. (No. 64513)	
Roncq.	3		Moved to Roncq.	
	5		Indent O/1440 for 2 Lewis Guns + 8 bags spare parts for 12 R.S. Fusiliers to replace lost.	
	7.		Indent O/1442 for one body Travelling Kitchen for 15th West Yorks to replace condemned. " O/1443 for one 18 pdr without Bm. to replace No 6125 condemned for serving for B/170 Bde. Received & issued to No 10 O.M. Workshop.	
Courtrai	8		Moved to Courtrai } Poor accommodation for Stores.	
Sweveghem	10		" " Sweveghem } Celebrated signing of armistice, news of which was received about 9 p.m. (21 hrs)	
	12		Two Lewis Guns received off indent O/1440 of 6th for 12 R.S.F.	
Pottelberg	15		Moved to Pottelberg. Indent O/1458 for two Kitchen Travelling Bodies for 24 R.S.F. to replace condemned	
	17		Indent O/1459 for various necessaries for returned P.O.W. Indent O/1461 for one wagon limbered G.S. to replace condemned for 31st Div. Signal Company	
	18		Indent O/1464 for one wagon G.S. to replace one abandoned in forward area for 31st DAC " O/1465 for one body Kitchen travelling for 11 E. Yorks to replace one abandoned in forward area.	

Instructions regarding War Diaries and Intelligence Summaries are contained in F. S. Regs., Part II. and the Staff Manual respectively. Title pages will be prepared in manuscript.

WAR DIARY
or
~~INTELLIGENCE~~ SUMMARY.

(Erase heading not required.)

Army Form C. 2118.

Place	Date	Hour	Summary of Events and Information	Remarks and references to Appendices
Pollelberg	21 Novr.		Indent O/1472 for one body kitchen travelling for 11 E. Yorks to replace condemned.	
S Omer.	25		Moved to Boulevard Strasbourg S. Omer. Ironclad store.	
	27.		Indent O/1477 for 40 tables, 80 forms for recreation rooms under Authority 5th Army administration No 28 of 19-11-18	
			W. Swallow Major Dados 31st Division	

A5834 Wt. W4973/M687 750,000 8/16 D. D. & L. Ltd. Forms/C.2118/13.

Instructions regarding War Diaries and Intelligence Summaries are contained in F. S. Regs., Part II. and the Staff Manual respectively. Title pages will be prepared in manuscript.

WAR DIARY
or
~~INTELLIGENCE SUMMARY.~~
(Erase heading not required.)

Army Form C. 2118.

DADOS 31 D
9/8 34

Place	Date	Hour	Summary of Events and Information	Remarks and references to Appendices
St Omer	Dec 1	1918	Indent O/1480 for 25 Stve. Sawyer to replace "V".	
	3		Indent O/1482 for 1 Cart O.M. to replace one abandoned in forward area for D/165 Bde R.F.A.	
			" O/1483 for 500 blankets urgently reqd for reinforcements.	
	9		Indent O/1485 for one body K. Travelling to replace Condemned for 18 D.L.I.	
	12		Indent O/1492 for one Cart water Tank to replace Condemned for B/165.	
	16		Indent O/1494 for one 18 pdr Carriage to replace No 14893 Condemned wear of B/170 Bde R.F.A.	
	17		Indent O/1495 for 1000 blankets - 3rd Blanket - Authority A.R.O. 3399 dated 15/12/18	
			O/1496 " one 18 pdr Carriage to replace No 35492 Condemned wear for B.165 R.F.A.	
	20		Indent O/1499 " 5000 blankets. Authority as 17th DADOS granted leave to 3.1.19	
	22		18 pdr carriage received at G.O.M.W. (Medium) for B/170 of indent O/1494 of 16.12.18	
	23		A.D.O.S. informed 10000 palliasses received for Division	
	25		18 pdr Carriage received of indent O/1496 of 17th inst for B/165	
	31		Indent O/1519 for one 18 pdr ... Bn to replace 4939 for C/165 } Authority	
			" O/1520 " " " " " " 1262 " C/170 } Q.M.G. 8128 (Q.O.1) 22/12/18	
			Units of the Division gradually bringing stores up to Mob. Table Strength. The Ordnance work greatly increased owing to the number of attached units	
			[illegible] Major DADOS 31 Div	

A5834 Wt. W4973/M687 750,000 8/16 D. D. & L. Ltd. Forms/C.2118/13.

www.ingramcontent.com/pod-product-compliance
Lightning Source LLC
Chambersburg PA
CBHW081431160426
43193CB00013B/2252